A
DURATION
MAN

A Staffordshire Soldier in the Great War

by

A J HERATY, RFA

YPRES, THE SOMME , PASSCHENDAELE and ITALY

CHURNET VALLEY BOOKS
43 Bath Street, Leek, Staffordshire. 01538 399033
email: picture.book@virgin.net website: freespace.virgin.net/c.hinton/

© The Estate of A J Heraty and Churnet Valley Books 1999
ISBN 1 897949 61 8

I have given my story the title 'A Duration Man', which were the terms upon which I enlisted to serve King and Country for the duration of the War.

I have named my first chapter The King's Shilling, which was the amount young men received when they enlisted in the forces in my day. The shilling constituted a day's pay, and was to be my pay for almost the next four years, one shilling per day including Sundays.

How I spent that fabulous amount of money, amounting to 7 shillings per week, I will explain as my story goes along.

This is a true and authentic story of my services in HM Forces in World War I, in which I served for almost four years in countries overseas, namely, Belgium, France and Italy, and in battles like the Battle of Ypres, the Battle of the Somme 1916, the Battle of Vimy Ridge, the great Battle of Passchendaele and Italy in 1918.

A J HERATY, RFA

Contents

Battle experiences subject of his book

IT took just 60 seconds and a brisk walk round the Town Hall, Newcastle, for Austin Heraty to age a whole year.

"It was a case of walking in aged 18, but coming out about half-an-hour later aged 19, and a new recruit for the Army fighting the 1914-18 war," Mr. Heraty remembers.

Mr. Heraty, who is 81 now and lives at 86, Stafford-crescent, Clayton, has vivid memories of "joining up," writes **Dianne Gibbons**.

"I didn't realise there was an age limit so when the officer asked my age I naturally said 18. It was then I realised I had to be 19. I felt very embarrassed about it and was just about to close the door feeling very sorry for myself when he called me back and said: 'Next time you come into this room you must be 19'.

"So just sixty seconds later, after walking the corridors of the Town Hall, I returned, said my age was 19, and I was in."

On joining the Army Mr. Heraty received the King's Shilling, which he, still has as one of his proud reminders of his war service. He also has all his medals, including the 1914-15 Star, the General Service Medal and the Victory Medal, and various records including date of enlistment and discharge.

With a great deal of v a l u a b l e information to hand from his experiences in famous battles including Ypres, Passchendaele and The Somme, Mr. Heraty is writing a book.

Mr. Heraty says that despite the fifty or so years that have elapsed since his service he can remember events that took place, vividly.

Terrible

He was wounded three times and didn't always wait to get well before going back into battle.

Fighting was more a matter of fact than choice, Mr. Heraty said. "We didn't really have any choice in the matter. We were all raw young men when we joined, but on our discharge we had really grown up, having witnessed many of the horrors of war.

"I said my prayers more when I went into the Army than before I joined up. I often said a little prayer to myself in the trenches when things looked so bleak. It was a comfort to me and seemed to help me."

In his book, Mr. Heraty tells of some of the terrible sights he witnessed as a teenage soldier.

"I saw people blown to pieces and a lot of them were my friends. You couldn't just pack up

though: you had to fight on. You didn't forget what you had seen or the friends you had lost but had your own survival to think of and your mates who were still lucky enough to be living."

Mr. Heraty said he had never regretted what he had done. "We were led to believe we were fighting for a good cause, for justice and for peace and that was very important to us all."

Mr. Heraty, who has two brothers, John aged 77 and Harold aged 64, said they were both delighted that he had decided to put his war memories into book form. "They are thrilled to bits."

Mr. Heraty thinks his book will revive a lot of interest in the war and hopes to hear from any veterans who fought with him at those battles.

"I think the book will put me in touch with people I haven't seen for half-a-century. I am housebound now but I still enjoy having visitors and reliving the old times."

FOREWORD
by Peter Lead

In his retirement, Austin James Heraty began to tell his children about his experiences in the First World War and fortunately his son, Tony, persuaded him to write them down, thinking that it would be an interest for his father and generally valuable to preserve his memories. Once it was written, the idea of getting it published was proposed, but this proved difficult as publishers then said it was rather short and perhaps too restricted in its appeal. Nevertheless, in 1979 articles appeared in the Evening Sentinel and another in the Daily Mail featuring Mr Heraty's wartime experiences.

Mr Heraty enlisted in the Royal Field Artillery in September 1915 and after initial training he was posted to "A' Battery, 80th Brigade RFA serving with the 17th (Northern) Division. At this time, the division formed part of V Corps, Second Army, and were located south-west of Ypres. Early in 1916, the division was involved in both the loss and recovery of the Bluff, a narrow ridge on the northern banks of the Ypres-Comines Canal, on 14th February and 2nd March respectively. During the great Somme offensive of July 1916, the division was involved in the capture of Fricourt and later in the fighting around Delville Wood where Mr. Heraty was wounded for the first time.

Evacuated back to England, he received treatment for his wounds at a military hospital in Newport, South Wales, before returning to France early in 1917. He did not rejoin his old unit but was posted to one of the RFA brigades serving with the 48th (South Midland) Division. During March and April of that year he witnessed the fighting withdrawal of the German army to the Hindenburg Line and the British occupation of the ruined town of Peronne. After a period of rest, his division was moved to the Ypres area where they were to take part in the battles collectively known as 'Third Ypres' or more popularly by the name of the last major objective Passchendaele. He took part in the battles for Langemarck, Polygon Wood, Broodseinde and Poelcappelle between August and October 1917. Again wounded, he heard at a Casualty Clearing Station that the 48th Division was to be sent to Italy where the war was going badly for our Italian allies.

The 48th Division began to entrain for Italy on 21st November and detrainment was completed around Legnago within ten days. At the beginning of March 1918, the division moved into the front line of the Montello Sector of the Piave Front, which it held until the middle of the month. In April they moved into reserve for the middle sector of the Asiago Plateau Front and saw action in the battle of the Piave on 15-16th June. Early in November, the division took part in the battle of Vittorio Veneto where they surrounded an Austrian army capturing four senior generals and about 14 battalions of soldiers. The next day the Armistice with Austria-Hungary came into effect and the fighting - not to mention Gunner Heraty's war - came to an end.

Now, eighty years after these events and nearly twenty years since Austin Heraty's death, his book is finally published. He tells a vivid story, the first hand account of a working man turned professional soldier. As might be expected it has little to say about the grand strategy and significance of the battles that he witnessed. His words are important because he describes the lice, mud, discomfort, cold and fear that all front-line soldiers endured during the long years of the war. Through him we become aware of the immense noise and physical toil accompanied by the horror of seeing comrades blasted away. He shares the relief that came through injury, of a rest behind the lines, the simple pleasure of having enough water for a shave, and a trip to the estaminet in a French town. It is, above all, a book of frightening horror and resigned courage.

The words he uses are not in anyway pretentious but his account makes fascinating and compelling reading. Happily the advances in computing and printing over the last twenty years have made the publication of this valuable account a viable proposition.

Austin James Heraty on left in 1916 after discharge from Newport Hospital.
Note wound stripe on the left arms.

THE SOLDIER'S NEXT-OF-KIN NOW LIVING.

Any change becoming known is to be duly noted, with the date of such change.

Note.—No entry on this page has any legal effect as a Will.

Nearest degree of relationship.		NAMES.	Latest known address to be given in full.
1st.	Wife.		
	Children.		
2nd.	Father.	Austin	15 Bailey Street Nuneaton Staffs
	Mother.		
3rd.	Brothers and Sisters.		
	Nephews and Nieces, if children of deceased brothers or sisters.		
4th.	Other relations.		

Signature of Soldier.

Regimental number. 107274

Signature of Commanding Officer, etc.

Date of Signature, 15-9-15

Adjutant No 1 Depot

† State whether brothers are younger or older.

SOLDIER'S NAME AND DESCRIPTION ON ATTESTATION.

(REGULAR FORCES.)

Name Austin James Keratty

Enlisted at Nuneaton

in the County of Staffs

on the 6-9-15

at the age of 19 years 2 months

for the term of Royal Artillery (R.H. & R.F.) for War years in the Army and years in the Reserve.

Born in the Parish of Nuneaton

in or near the Town of Staff

in the County of Staff

Trade or calling Bicycle Maker

Last permanent residence 15 Bailey St, Nuneaton Staffs

Height 5 feet 7 inches

Complexion Fair Hair Black

Eyes Grey

Marks

* Religion

† Signature of Soldier

* This should be described under one of the following denominations, viz.:— "Church of England," "Presbyterian," "Wesleyan," "Baptist," or "Congregational," other Protestant denomination (name of denomination to be noted), "Roman Catholic" or "Jew."

† Whenever a Soldier who cannot write makes his mark in acknowledgment of having received pay or allowances, etc., such mark is to be witnessed by the signature of a witness (other than the pay-sergeant).

Page from the "Soldiers' Small Book".

Chapter 1
The King's Shilling

On the 16th September 1915 I had returned from work at about 2.30pm from what we called the day shift. I was employed as a benzole maker in the by-product plant at Apedale, owned by the Midland Coal, Coke and Iron Company Ltd, and in those days the pattern seemed to be get your dinner, get your bath, put on your clothes, or as we said, your glad rags, and go off out to meet your girlfriend or your pal, whichever suited a young man of 18 years.

I was as green as grass. I had decided to go out and meet my pal early that evening. He was a shift worker like myself, but he worked underground in the coal mines as an electrician, so we were both able to fit in with each other's time for our various escapades. Before I introduce my pal I will tell you that the names and places mentioned in my story are all correct and true. My pal's name was Absolam Hackney. He lived at 24 Chapel Street, Knutton, and it was he that I met the evening my story begins.

We met in Newcastle-under-Lyme and we were walking down Liverpool Road with not a care in the world, as young men of our age appeared to be in those days. We were really at a loose end that evening. We might go to a local dance hall or to the pictures. Newcastle could boast a cinema and a small music hall. My first job from school was at the cinema, the Newcastle Cinema, which was opened in May 1910 by the London Cinematograph Co, and I was paid the handsome amount of 5/- per week as an usherette. We were all boys then, and we would conduct patrons to their seats.

The small music hall was where 'Dratigan' (real name Ernest Beresford), the first man in the world to 'loop the loop' on a bicycle, finished up after his last performance at the Kings Hall. Ernest was a great personal friend of mine, with whom I was to work for a number of years after the Great War. But back to the things my pal and I were talking about - Picture Theatres. We were getting towards the end of Liverpool Road when Abe said,

"Suppose we go the pictures tonight for a change, Austin."

"What film are they showing there tonight?"

I think he said something about Ronald Coleman in 'Under Two Flags', or some film about the Foreign Legion, and I remarked it seemed rather a bit too stuffy to go sitting in a cinema on a nice evening like this. Our conversation turned to some of our other pals, who had decided to join up in

Apedale Iron and
Coal Works.

The Newcastle
Cinema.

Courtesy of Barry Blaize.

the Army or Navy. Then it happened.

I said to Abe, "What about you and I enlisting in the Army?"

Quite a lot of our pals had joined some branch of the forces, you see, and we were beginning to miss them. The Country was still only calling for volunteers because the government had not passed the law for conscription yet. However, since I was the type of person who would have a go at anything once, and I was very interested in the things we might see and experience over there in France, I said again to Abe, "Come on, let's go and enlist".

We went along through Red Lion Square into the High Street and to the Town Hall, which was being used as the local enlisting depot. Actually the room being used was the room for juvenile court cases. Abe led the way through into the Old Town Hall. We followed a large notice with an arrow pointing to the right, and we were in.

Abe went first and as I followed I got my first glimpse of what a recruiting office looked like. There were two persons sitting behind a long table at the far end of the room. One of them was the Worshipful Mayor of the Borough of Newcastle, who was William Mellard, or Bert Mellard as most people called him, and the other person was the Listing Sergeant, a colour sergeant I was told later, not that I knew the difference, one from the other. As I told you before, I was as green as grass regarding anything connected with Army rules and regulations - and we are just about to walk into the long grass!

Abe was the first up to the table and I stood behind him with my ears open and my 'L' plates on, and the swearing-in began. The Listing Sergeant was the person who was to put the questions. The Mayor, who came from over the street facing the Town Hall (Mellard and Sons, Ironmongers), held a watching brief while the Sergeant put the questions, which went as follows:

Sergeant to Abe; "Name please?".

"A. Hackney, 24 Chapel Street, Knutton".

"Age?"

"22 years of age."

Abe was told to part strip off and get on the scales.

My humble self was next to face the Sergeant with, "Name, please?"

"Austin J. Heraty, 15 Bailey Street, Newcastle."

"Age?"

"18, Sir".

The Sergeant looked up at me and said "Did you say 18, Mr Heraty?"

I said, "Yes, sir".

There was a few moments silence in the room and I stood there like a

The centre of Newcastle under Lyme, Staffordshire, showing the Guild Hall ("old Town Hall") in the early years of the twentieth century.

Another contemporary view of Newcastle under Lyme.

spare dinner. Still nobody spoke and I felt so embarrassed I just turned around and began to walk out of the chamber, but before I could close the door behind me, someone called out, "Come back here!"

Of course, it was the Listing Sergeant. I walked back to the table and the Sergeant said to me again, "How old did you say you were, Mr Heraty?"

Still the penny had not dropped. I said, "18, Sir."

The Sergeant looked up at me and said "I am sorry Mr Heraty, but I will tell you what to do. You can have a walk around town, but if you come into this room again tonight, you must be 19 years of age."

And then the penny did drop. I was around the Town Hall in about 60 seconds flat, and was in the room before my pal Abe had got off the scales. I went through a repeat of the previous questions - "name", etc.

"19 years of age, Sir."

And I was in! Signed and received the King's shilling. But before we left the chamber, we asked the Listing Sergeant if he would grant us leave of absence for 7 days, so we could be at home for Newcastle Wakes which was the following week. He agreed and told us to report to Stoke-on-Trent on 13th September, 1915.

Talk about Dad's Army! Little did I realise how far I was to be from that phrase during the four years which were to follow.

Well, we were proud of ourselves; the following few days we were delighted to pass the news on to all our friends that we had decided to join up and go to fight for King and Country, and most of all, to our girl friends who, part glad and part sorry, agreed that the young men of the country were duty bound to go and do their bit, as the saying was.

To finish off the excitement of that evening we called in at the Star, in the Ironmarket, and had a couple of pints, then off home to prepare for work next day. We usually had to get up as early as 5.00am to get to work by 6.00am. So for next few days we decided to make the best of our freedom in Civvy Street.

Our first job, of course, was to give notice to our employers to terminate our jobs at our respective 'plants'. Although it was less than a full week's notice, our employers did not object because it was not only a good reason for leaving the job, but it also put the employers on the list as having made sacrifices of manpower to help King and Country. In fact they paid us up at the weekend (including a week's pay in hand) which made us pretty flush for the last few days of our freedom and we made the best of it.

As most of North Staffordshire knows, our Wakes Week was our annual holiday and was called Stoke Wakes, which really was held in Hanley. That

Duration of War Enlisted 6. 9 15   161.

Army Form B. 216.

RECRUITING.
PASS FOR RECRUITS.

Name of Recruit in full _Austin James Heraty_

Attested for the _R F A_ Regt., Corps, or General Service.

Proceeding by **NORTH STAFFORD** Railway or _____ Steamship.

From **STOKE-ON-TRENT** To _Lichfield_

To join the _R. F. A._ (Regt. or Depot) at _____

Has received his ticket by the **NORTH STAFFORD.** Railway or _____ Steamship.

DESCRIPTION of Recruit.		
Apparent Age	19 years	2 months.
Height	5 feet	7 inches.
Complexion _fresh_	Eyes	_Grey_
Hair _Black_	Dress	_Plain_

Whether in possession of a Great Coat.	Whether Ration allowance for the day of journey has been paid him.	Amount of allowance for the journey paid him, if any.	Actual fare of passage paid.
	Yes		Date _13. 9. 15_

Signature of Officer sending the Recruit. Name _____ Rank _Wirrall Capt._

N.B.—It is requested that the bearer of this Pass, should he by accident miss his passage, may receive assistance, to forward him to his destination, from all Police authorities, Railway officials, and Officers of steamships.

The description given above is furnished in order to prevent an improper use of this Pass.

Any report of irregularity should be addressed to the Secretary, War Office, London, S.W.

MEMO.—This Pass must be given to each Recruit as soon as he takes his seat in the train, or embarks, with instructions to be careful to deliver it, on arrival at his destination, to the Serjeant who meets him; if from the distance to be travelled he receives subsistence beyond the date of starting, it should be stated.

(8·82·68) W 1953—27 100,000 7/14 H W V Forms
4581—515 140,000 9/14 B. 216
38

Army Railway Pass.

Pat Collins Fair came to the Wakes every year.

The Old Star, Newcastle under Lyme.

was then followed by Burslem Wakes, or as locals called it, "Boslem Wakes", the town and its surroundings made famous by Arnold Bennett, the great novelist who was born in the town of Burslem.

The paraphernalia of the show man, including the roundabouts, the hobby horses, and side shows (owned chiefly by Pat Collins), came to Newcastle, for our Wakes, from Burslem. As mentioned above, we had the choice of one picture theatre, one music hall and Newcastle Wakes on our last weekend, and of course the last named won and we were down at the Fair Ground with the boys and girls each night on the gondolas and steam boats until our last night at home came along. (The Wakes were held down at the Smithfield at that time).

Then we had to pack, which did not take long as we left our best togs at home and travelled casual to the Recruiting Office at Stoke-on-Trent, to report on the 13th September, 1915. On arrival we just had to produce our Attestation Papers to the Sergeant in Charge, who was expecting us, and who put one or two questions to us, in the army style now, and gave us a Railway Warrant. He told us we were to catch a train at Stoke Station where a travel ticket would be issued for us to proceed to Lichfield. We were on our way to a war which I for one did not know the first thing about.

We had said our goodbyes to our parents and brothers and sisters that morning, and my Dad, who at the time was in the teaching profession - he was Assistant Head Master at Wellington Road School in Hanley - accompanied Abe and me to Stoke Station.

I mention my Dad's profession because it was to stand me in good stead for this story in the later years of the War. He kept all my records, including all the correspondence from the War Office in the familiar buff forms, which informed my parents each time I was wounded. This was on three separate occasions, namely the Battle of the Somme, the Battle for Vimy Ridge and then again in Italy during the "Big Push" in 1918.

At Stoke Station we were to catch our train for Lichfield, which happened to be the London train that ran from Manchester, calling at Stoke at 9.50am each morning and making its next stop at Lichfield. There were quite a number of young men on the platform, each with a small suitcase or parcel, and each on the same errand as ourselves. We were not kept waiting long before our train steamed in and we were on our way to Lichfield.

Our journey was uneventful except that we met another young man, who turned out to be the son of a butcher at Silverdale, by the name of Allman. We would all cling together during the following weeks, until we were separated by drafting to various units. I was to lose my regular pal Abe

Hackney at the barracks of the Northumberland Fusiliers, Newcastle-upon-Tyne, and from that time onwards, in nearly four years of war overseas, I only met one man out of the whole of Staffordshire that I knew, which seems incredible.

The train steamed on through Trentham, Stone and Colwich towards Lichfield. As it drew to a halt at the station we could hear the loudspeakers calling out, *"All passengers who are bound for Whittington Barracks will they please fall in outside the station entrance"*. I was about to lose my identity as a civilian and become 107274 Gunner A. J. Heraty, R.F.A.

There were about 25 of us, all young men, who filed out of the station, where a Corporal, who seemed to be an old soldier, was standing.

"Now, boys", he said, "Just form into twos and pick up your bags and follow me."

We were quite taken by surprise at the nice way in which he told us what to do. (Of course, we were beginners, which we soon found out later.)

We started off to our new home through the City of Lichfield, with its three magnificent spires, and on our way to Whittington Barracks, which seemed a hell of a way then but was only about two or three miles walk.

We arrived there just before lunch time and after checking in we were taken to a room in the barracks and the Corporal showed us to our beds (which were Army style of course), and told us where the cookhouse was and where to find the recreation room, etc. We were then given a meal and the Corporal told us we could roam about the Barracks within reasonable bounds, but we were not allowed out.

Of course we soon found out that 'Orders is Orders', in the Army vocabulary, but we were not put out because our new surroundings were all so strange to us that this took up a lot of our time.

To our surprise it was to end sooner than any of us realised. When we assembled on the square before our tea parade we were told again that we were confined to barracks that evening and then informed that the following morning we were to entrain for our new depot, which was to be Newcastle-upon-Tyne. So in less than 24 hours we were sent from Newcastle to Newcastle, which was to be the place of our training for soldiers of war.

The journey to Newcastle-upon-Tyne was a long and tedious one, up through the east coast into Yorkshire and Northumberland, through Gateshead, over the 'high level' and the River Tyne into Newcastle. I think it took us between 4 and 5 hours to travel all the way up north and it was a new experience for me to travel a long distance by rail, or even by any other means at that time. Our wages at work were very low and after paying our dues at home there was not much left to allow for touring around or going for a holiday at the seaside. My journey up north was new and interesting to me, travelling through the countryside and passing through places like Huddersfield, Leeds, Darlington, until we finally arrived at Newcastle.

Athough the journey was tedious, everything was new to us, which helped to break the monotony, and we arrived in good shape and cheerfulness. As we travelled up from Lichfield we made quite a number of stops on the way, and we must have picked up a lot of new 'faces' in the form of new recruits. When we arrived at Newcastle our party had increased to about 150 when we were all paraded outside the station, incidentally, by another Corporal.

I was beginning to think the Corporals had to do all the work of the NCOs, but you learn as you go along. From now on we were under orders - and what I learned as we went along was that the best thing was to obey all orders -especially the last one - in the Army. The NCO in charge of us soon got us to arrange ourselves in fours and we proceeded to march through the town.

After we had travelled about 1½ miles we came to a place called St James's Hall. This was to be our first billet, and I thought it was a bit rough at the time (a thin straw palliasse on the floor of the hall with a couple of Army blankets per man and that was your bed), but in my later chapters you will see that I was to wish many a time I had a nice clean floor to sleep on, instead of under the hedge or in a shell hole.

We soon sorted ourselves out and each of us were told by the NCO to claim a palliasse on the floor. As we were still in Civvies, with as yet no Army kit to bother about, we soon had our blankets spread over it to complete our beds, and we put our odds and ends on the top, to stake our claim.

After the sorting out of small parcels and suitcases we were eventually all settled with a bed each, and after the commotion had subsided, we were told to assemble in the centre of the Hall in two rows. The NCO then told us we were to call numbers out starting at the right, such as 1-2-3-4 etc, which was, I assume, a kind of roll call to make sure he had not lost any us on the way from the station. After he had found us all correct he began to tell us in detail our orders for the remainder of the day, adding that he trusted we would obey all instructions as he was responsible for our behaviour until we were dismissed or handed over to another NCO.

From now on we were really under orders. Although our NCO was very kind and fatherly towards us still, we were, to say the least, just raw recruits a few hours old. We soon realised we were to do as we were told and follow the crowd. Our man in charge told us to fall in outside the Hall and that he was going to march us up through the part of town we came to know later as Gallowgate, and which was to be our rendezvous for several weeks to come and our cookhouse during our stay in Newcastle.

Our NCO was taking us to have our tea at what turned out to be a combination of small workshops and warehouses which the government had commandeered for war purposes, to billet and feed new recruits. It was situated just above Gallowgate and was owned by a firm known as Scott and Turners, who were the originators of Andrews Liver Salts, which we were told had just come onto the market.

When we were assembled in the canteen our man in charge told us that after our tea we were free to go and look around town, but we were to be back at St James by 10.00pm. which was 'lights out' - and woe betide the man who gets locked out. After we had finished our tea, Abe and I decided to have a look around, to get to know the place which was going to be our abode, living and training, during the coming weeks, and which I will do my best to describe.

We found our way down through Gallowgate and into the centre of town, which brought us to Grainger Street, at the time the chief shopping centre of the town. The shops were full of everything you could mention and it took us a good two hours just browsing the windows and the side shows. You could spend hours looking through shop windows, and also a lot of money if you happened to be flush.

We managed to find our way down towards the River Tyne to have a look at both the High Level and Low Level bridges, which to us Midlanders seemed a wonderful sight, because we could not boast of having any high bridges or wide rivers in our part of the county. After a quick look around we began to retrace our steps back to St. James Hall, calling in for a couple of pints on the way.

It was now about 9.00pm and we decided to get back to our billet before lights out. Actually we arrived at the Hall about 9.30pm and after chatting a while with our new pals about where we had been and what we had seen during the evening, time soon rolled on to 10.00pm.

A few moments later our Corporal came into the Hall and called out, "Now, fellows, will you all stand by you beds and be counted". He walked up one side and down the other. "Fine," he said, "all present and correct and do not forget, tomorrow morning - Reveille, 7.00am sharp." He blew his whistle like a referee, as being new recruits we could not afford a bugler, and that was 'lights out'.

Next morning arrived all too early after our first night on the boards, and most of us began to realise 'there was no place like home'. Gone were the feather beds and mother's cooking. We were in the army now. At 7.00am prompt the old Corporal came strutting along the Hall calling out "Now chaps, come on, show a leg", which was the old army way of telling you to get out of bed and get dressed.

After the NCO had allowed us about five minutes to get ship-shape, he told the party to fall in outside and arrange ourselves into two lines. He gave the order, "Right turn" and we were on our way to Gallowgate, and Scott and Turners, which was to be our billet, for ablutions and cookhouse, for the next few weeks. As it turned out those few weeks were shorter than we thought.

After a good douche in cold water and a quick brush up we were led into the canteen for breakfast, and oh boy, did it taste good; bacon, sausage; one would think we had not eaten anything for a week the way we cleaned our plates. And I would like to add it was the best smoked bacon that we got, which we never seemed to get in Civvy Street. I can definitely say that throughout my army career I never tasted better bacon than the troops were fed on. Incidentally, bacon will crop up again later in my story, once or twice, because we were to learn, as we went, on that a soldier's main ration during the war - when we could get it - was 'half a loaf and a dip in the fat', put in army terms. Before we had finished with it all, we were to experience days when the bread ration used to run to a small loaf of bread between as many as thirty men, and in the winter time, when it was frozen and covered with mud, we had to split it up with a billhook.

To get back to Scott and Turners; the NCO had us all lined up outside, then we are marched along Gallowgate and up the Fenning Road to the barracks of the Northumberland Fusiliers, and across the square to the Quartermaster's stores. We were still in civvies, but not for long now. We passed along through the stores, with various soldiers standing behind counters to give us one short glance and hand over a tunic or breeches, and moved along to the next counter where we got socks and boots, knife, fork and spoon, etc., then further for cap and cap badge, also a pair of spurs, which of course had the army jargon of Mark 1 or Mark 2 or 3, and not forgetting puttees, which all Gunners and Drivers had to wear, along with the spurs. The look which the soldier gave you from behind the counter seemed to say to you that the 'clobber' he had just dished out to you had got to fit, 'or else', including the boots.

After signing for the various kit and equipment we had just received, we were all marched off across the barracks, by a short cut, to a place known as

Leeses Park, which was all dotted over with 'hutments' to billet troops, and was to be our home for the coming weeks during our training. Each hut had a compartment for 30 to 40 beds and when we arrived each party was told of their own particular hut, and then there was a general rush for a bed and a space for bedding, bearing in mind that each group of pals tried to get near each other. By the time we had all got into the hut with all our clobber we began to wonder whether the NCO had sent two parties to the same hut. But the real fun was to start later, when each man was trying on his new 'clobber'. Some of the tunics were more suitable for a pregnant woman and some were too long or too short in the sleeves. I do not think any of us knew how to start the puttees off, whether from the ankle or the knee. The result was a lot of swopping and changing, until eventually we began to look something look soldiers.

We were all anxious to get dressed up and get down into the town, hoping of course to look like soldiers who had been in the army about five years instead of just five minutes. We really did fancy our chances with our smart breeches and spurs on, thinking everybody was looking at us and saying, "There goes some nice lads!".

Now I could really say I was 107274 Gunner A J Heraty, R.F.A.

Gateshead at the exit from the high level bridge.

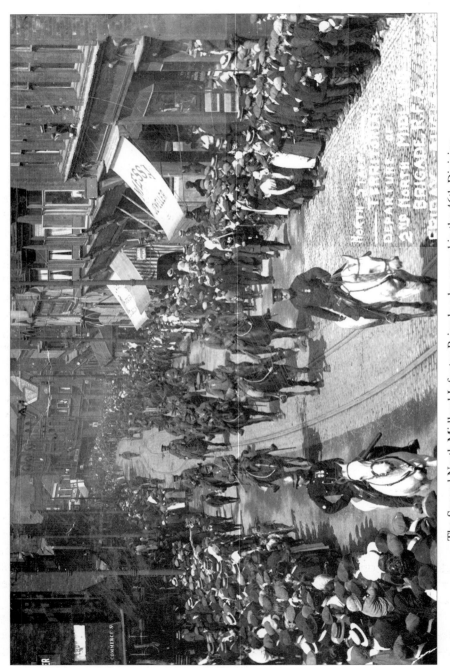

The Second North Midland Infantry Brigade who served in the 46th Division.

Chapter 2
Square-bashing and Guns

From now on we really were under orders and we realised we must submit to being disciplined and take our orders from the NCOs or Officers, as the case may be, whether on parade, or off parade. Even though some of the orders given might be stupid or wrong, you were always duty bound to obey the last order given to you in the Army.

After a very few weeks and many miles of square bashing we began to get accustomed to the Sergeant or Sergeant Major calling out, "Quick march right turn, left turn, on the double, halt, about turn, quick march! If you broke your mother's heart you won't break mine, on the double, etc", and on it went for day after day, week after week, until we began to feel and look like soldiers. In the meantime we became accustomed to the army systems, doing everything on time. What with the exercises and P.T. training we began to develop appetites like horses and one was always glad to hear the bugle call "Come to the cookhouse door, boys". The day's routine was: Reveille at 06.30hrs, dinner at 12.30hrs, tea at 16.30hrs, supper at 20.00hrs, if you wanted any, and lights out at 22.00hrs; and woe betide any new recruit trying to sneak in after 22.00hrs; he was for the 'high jump' or guard room for report, which meant a week's CB - confined to barracks.

After your tea break, any time about 17.00hrs, you were free for the remainder of the day until lights out at 22.00hrs, unless you were detailed for guard duty, which came round every two to three weeks. As we were still new to the army game we began to try and spruce ourselves up with the old spit and polish to make ourselves look like regular soldiers, ready to go down into town to chat up the girls.

Of course everything seemed new to us up here in the north of England. The strange dialect of the Geordies, as they are called, and most of all the hospitality which we were shown by the Geordies. I do not think I ever met any better people in my life. After we had been up there for two weeks we became used to the routine of smartening up for the evening visit into town, cleaning buttons and boots, not forgetting our spurs. We spent the evenings in the usual ways, but there was no pub crawling, as they termed it, because we could not afford to.

I omitted to tell you that as we got our clobber from the store we were issued with a pay book and a 'small book' that all soldiers know about, which contains the rules and regulations concerning the army, and also a form of will to be made out by the soldier in case he was 'knocked out'. I may add here and now, that it did not take me long to make mine, because my assets at the time were nil. I was able to make a weekly allotment to my mother of sixpence per day, which cut my pay by half, and I would now soldier for three shillings and sixpence per week for the remainder of the War.

I had saved a bob or two when we left home to come up to the barracks at Newcastle-on-Tyne. When we found out there was a tailor in the barracks we were all in a rush to have our tunics taken in at the waist to make us look as smart as the old soldiers and take that new raw look off us. We were now allowed to start our training on the guns as there were not too many guns to share at that time.

Although we could boast of having a complete battery of four guns, 18 pounders, we had to commence our training on the old 15 pounders which belonged to the RHA and which carried the No 1 dial sight then. But after the previous couple of weeks' square-bashing and route marches, it was quite a change, and I for one found it very interesting. I was soon spotted out by the Sergeant as being a lad who would make a good gunner.

We now had drill morning and afternoon, as well as learning our part numbers on the gun in position. We soon got to learn that the Sergeant was No. 1, who was always at the trail eye to take orders from his superior officer. No. 2 was the man who set the range for the gun, No. 3 was the gun layer, No. 4 rammed the shell up the breech which had been already opened by No. 2; and No. 5 and No. 6 were employed on the corrector bar, which was used to work out the timing of the fuse on the nosecap of the shell and was passed to No. 4 for loading in the gun.

After about a week on the old 15 pounders we were switched to the 18 pounders, which was to be my type of gun throughout the War. The 18 pounder was a more sophisticated gun - the dial sight was a patent stolen from the Germans, I am told. Early in the War it was a form of periscope, as well as a dial sight, and it enabled the gun layer to use the aiming post at the rear of the gun instead of the one at the front.

As our training began to hot up a bit, I was beginning to be picked out as a good No. 3, for being the gun layer, and my pal Abe was spotted on the next gun as also being quite suitable as a No. 3. A couple of weeks later we were both awarded our proficiency badges as gun layers and were allowed to have the latter stitched on the lapels of our tunics. (Open the window and let me throw my chest out!)

By this time we were beginning to look like artillery men and they started to take us out on to the town moor for real training with horses, limbers and guns, to prepare for real action stations. Boy, did we feel proud of ourselves, with harnesses and guns gleaming in the sun, and galloping over the town moor, swinging into action like the real thing. This was to continue over the next few weeks, and in the meantime we were detailed for vaccination; most of us went through the mill during the next ten days or so. I felt sorry for a lot of the young lads who had not been vaccinated at birth, which a lot of parents had failed to have done, although it was compulsory. Some of the poor buggers had arms like legs and swollen fingers like arms, but we were allowed to wear a red band around our arms as an indication to the rough ones, to prevent them from bumping us about, and that helped a lot.

Within a few days we were as right as rain again, plus the fact that we had missed a turn on guard duty helped. Now we were back to square one, only this time we had to have training in the riding school and learn to ride a horse, to bump the saddle as they say, which resulted in a few sore backsides. Then it was back to the square for more P.T. and square bashing.

At the close of the day our evenings did not vary much after tea; poshing up, cleaning buttons, boots and spurs, and out on the town, which we were getting to know very well now, strutting down the Fenning Road into Gallowgate, up and down Grainger Street and then along the Scotswood Road towards the big Swan Hunter shipyards, where thousands of people were employed.

Other evenings we would cross over the High Level bridge and the Tyne into Gateshead. At that period the bridge was like a toll gate. You had to pay a penny to cross over the bridge and as far as I can remember vehicles had to pay threepence or sixpence according to their size. In Gateshead we used to go to a beauty spot called Low Fell; the walks and the scenery were a treat for the eyes.

It was usually on Sunday evenings that we chose to visit this beauty spot, which reminds me that I have not told you what we did with our Sundays off. Our first problem was to dodge the church parade, for whether you were C. of E. or R.C. you were expected to line up for church parade, and the NCO in charge would come around and inspect inside all the hutments to see if anybody was swinging the lead. Unless you had a good alibi such as cookhouse fatigues, or you were sick, then you were for the high jump, so we had to be a bit slick and dodgy. Every hut had a door at each end, so we spied our chance as the NCO came out of the hut next door after inspecting it - a case of, as one door opens another door shuts! We switched from one hut to the other before you could say Jack Robinson, waited about ten minutes for the parade to move off and we were free. Free for what? Well,

Newcastle from Gateshead.

Artillery recruits.

our Sunday morning destination was the quayside, down on the River Tyne.

The trams were running in those days, but we could not afford even that small fare on our three shillings and sixpence per week. Anyway, the walk did us good and we were down at the quayside in about half an hour. Talk about London's Petticoat Lane, the quayside could run a good second. You could buy anything there, almost, from a pin to an elephant. There was a tipster they called One-eyed Scotty. The goods they sold went very cheap and a lot were sold by Dutch auction, which means starting at the top and coming down until someone decides to have a go and buy. Naturally, we held a watching brief on all the buying and selling but it was great fun as a lot of the stallholders were real comics.

After our morning tour down at the river we would decide to make our way back to Leese's Park, which joined the south side of the barracks. Both were adjacent to St James Park, the football ground of Newcastle United. We now arrived back at our billet, at just about 12.30 and in time for our dinner, after which we were still free for the remainder of the day. After browsing through the Sunday paper it was time for us to do the usual job of smartening up in readiness for our evening visit to Gateshead and Low Fell. Time to put the shine on buttons, boots and spurs, plus the whitening of our lanyards with blanco. The lanyard was worn around the left shoulder and was used in the old days for firing the old type of cannon. We spent the evening in a very enjoyable manner, meeting lots of nice girls, chatting along with them. We really were on top of the world!

But things were to change in the very near future, changes that would cause a lot of silent tears and great disappointment, and would go with me throughout the long years of the War. My troubles were just about to begin. We had now been in the army for about five weeks and it was Monday morning again, with P.T. and gun - but mostly guns now, because I think our Sergeant had been given instructions to hot it up a bit. Over in France they were waiting for reinforcements. We had lost a lot of men in the battles around Ypres.

A few days later we were called together on a special parade ordered by our C.O. We had already been told that men of certain trades were being sorted out from our ranks, to be kept back for industrial purposes. We were also told that they were beginning to up the names of men who would be picked out for the new drafts to go overseas. As both Abe and myself were in protected trades at that time, Abe as an electrician and me as a benzole maker, it would be possible for us to dodge the drafts and stay behind. Now as I was very keen and was full of the desire to go overseas to see France and what the War was like, I talked it over with my pal Abe and won him over, as I thought.

We both decided, when it came to our turn on the parade ground, to tell the officer in charge that we were labourers. My pal and I were in the front ranks and Abe was about a dozen men away from me to my right. The officer who was making the enquiries seemed to spend quite a time talking to my pal Abe. The reason, as I found out later at the weekend, was although I had stuck to my promise and told the officer when he arrived down the line that I was a labourer, and he soon dealt with me, Abe had doubled-crossed me and admitted to the officer that he was an electrician.

It all came out at the weekend. Abe was posted up as going to Immingham Docks for the rewiring of ships and I was posted up on the list for a draft overseas to France. I was given seven days embarkation leave and I never saw him again until the War was over. I had been in the army now for six weeks and was passed out as a first class gunlayer for overseas. It was an indication of how keen I had been to learn and understand the workings of an 18 pounder gun.

I was now on my seven days leave, which seemed to fly by too quickly, but I did have the opportunity to go to one or two shows, including Henry the Fifth at the Theatre Royal, Hanley, and also a variety show at the Grand Theatre, Hanley. I visited my old works at Apedale, seeing a lot of my old pals who made a big fuss of me and showered all manner of treats on me. But as I said, the days seemed to fly by and I was soon on my way to the Northumberland Fusiliers Barracks at Newcastle-on-Tyne again - a day late, for which I was expecting Jankers or a week's C.B.

I had to go before the C.O. for sentence but as I was to be drafted overseas in a couple of days he let me off with a caution. My pal Abe had already been sent to the Docks on the East Coast to work on the ships so I was a loner now, and was to stay that way all through the War. Many were the times between then and now I have had the symptoms of home-sickness. I could only say 'San Fairy Ann', as the Welsh people say. Now all I was waiting for was the next couple of days to slip by before I would be on my way to the War in France.

Departure day soon arrived and with all our kit bags packed up we were lined up outside the barracks in rows four deep, and marched down to the Central Station, Newcastle, onto a through train to Southampton Docks, where we joined a few thousand more troops. We were led aboard an old tramp steamer; there must have been several thousand of us. You've heard of sardines in a tin, well this old ship should have been called the Sardinia. To

The new Immingham Docks.

The Grand, Hanley.

make it worse we were all issued with the old cork life-jackets to wear, as we sailed out of Southampton Docks to Le Havre. The journey across the Channel took five or six hours and we were in semi-darkness because of submarines and enemy aircraft.

There were very few of us who had been to sea before and the old boat was loaded enough to put her right down on the water line. With a heavy swell and rough seas and the boat diving, rising and rolling, quite a lot of the lads were seasick. The lavatories were out of bounds because we were so crowded on the decks. We were all like learners on an ice-rink! But we arrived safely in the port of Le Havre, and following a lot of running about by the officers and NCOs, we were allowed to disembark onto the quayside, where, after much scrambling, we managed to get a cup of tea or a dixie of soup. After an hour or so the Sergeants and the Sergeant Majors began to shout out for certain units to fall in here and such a squad to fall in there, and it did not take them very long to sort us all out.

The train to take us up through the north of France was a long one, composed of old carriages and horse boxes. As part of our contingent marched off to board the train there was a general rush for the carriages and the Devil take the hindmost, as they say. I was fortunate enough to get into a carriage, although unlike the English trains there was no upholstery, just plain seats and no cushions even, but as we had a long journey ahead of us on that old train, it was better than being in a horse box.

At last we settled in and the train began to move out of the docks slowly - and I mean slowly. As we were to learn in the years that followed, the French had only two speeds on their railways - slow and stop. We could, for example, drop out of our carriage, run up to the front of the train, turn a tap on the side of the engine and get a can of hot water to brew a cup of tea! Hour after hour we chugged onwards across northern France, passing through some nice countryside and places like Rouen, Montreuil, which was the general headquarters of the British Expeditionary Forces at that time, and then on to Etaples, skirting by Boulogne then turning east and up through Cassells and into a little town by the name of Poperinghe where, along with several other ranks, I was posted to 'A' Battery, 80th Bgde, 17th Division. This was to be my billet throughout the months that followed, and the town of Poperinghe was between three and four miles from the battlefield front of Ypres, where I was to get my first baptism in the horrors of war.

To Britain on Leave—To France on Service

The caption to this First World War magazine tells of the great moment when two troop ships cross, one taking new recruits out, the other bringing soldiers home, and a great cheer goes out from both boats.

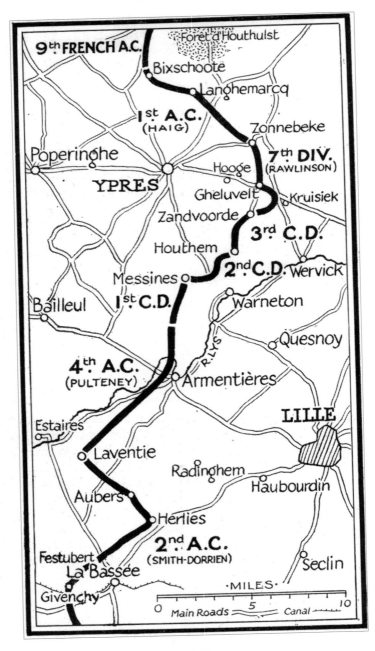

The British line at Ypres

Chapter 3
The Menin Gate and Ypres

After many hours and many stops we arrived at the little station of Poperinghe, but long before we reached there, we could hear the sound of gunfire reverberating through the atmosphere like thunder in the distance - a sound we became used to in the years that followed. There were only about 150 left on the train at the last stop, as we had detrained a lot of various units on the way up. They lined us up on the platform and the Sergeant in charge began to call out the names from various lists he had. So many to the 7th Division, or to the 46th Division, and about 20 names including one NCO in our party, to be sent as reinforcements to 'A' Battery, 17th Division, 80th Brigade, about a mile away, just off the main road to Ypres. Here there was an old farmyard comprised of sheds, barns and other outbuildings. This was to be our billet for a few months to come.

There were two things we learnt during that first week; apart from the mud that is. The horses were to be watered and fed before anyone else each morning - and we were as lousy as any of the other troops at the billet. This was the silent enemy - to my mind a damn sight worse than the mud and the muck, and only just second to the shelling and torture of war. The bunks in our barn were all handmade from a bit of 3 by 2 built in a two tier system with wire netting stretched across them. Of course army rules and regulations never let up - or down for that matter. It was reveille each morning at 6.30am and we had to fall in, walking along duck boards to a bit of drier ground; if you missed your step and fell off the duck boards you could easily drop into the mud up to your waist. Each battery in a brigade was a four gun battery and was made up of four 'subsections', namely, A,B,C,D; I was posted to 'A' subsection. By what appeared to be a mere coincidence, whenever we fell in on parade at each roll call, I always seemed to be in the rear ranks behind a fellow named Townsend, who was the lousiest man in the battery. You could see the lice, big grey and black ones, crawling around the collar of his tunic, and down his neck; but he didn't care a damn. I have seen him, on more occasions than one can imagine, put his hand through his tunic and into his shirt and pull one out, and if it was not been big enough he put the bloody thing back again!

Before long we were just as lousy as he was and we were writing back home for 'Harrison's Pomade, which helped to kill some of the buggers off, but we soon found a better way. This was to take your shirt off, get a lighted candle and run the seams of your shirt through the naked flame. Talk about machine guns, you could hear the buggers pop all through the barn. Now I know one can smell bugs and even cockroaches, which both have an earthy smell, but the lice were the silent enemy. Later in my story I will tell about another man who was the cleanest man in the battery, a fellow by the name of Campbell.

By this time we had been in the army about eight weeks, but we were not singled out to do any special duties yet, like the older ones, such as going up to the 'gun positions' at Ypres with rations and ammunitions. Instead we were given plenty of 'fatigues', such as grooming the mud off the horses or cleaning the mud from our billet and around the barns.

We had plenty of 'rations' at that period to feed us up. In fact, quite a lot of food was wasted; I have seen half cheeses thrown on the muck heap, and a lot of troops had saved up all their tins of jam and marmalade and built up a dug-out with them. There were tins of 'bully beef' chucked in a heap, 'Libby's' and 'Fray Bentos', which were to become collector's pieces before the War was over!

We got our first contact with the War the day we arrived at the wagon lines just in front of the town of Poperinghe. The Germans, or 'Jerry', used to bombard them for about half an hour, around 11.00am every morning, with a long range gun which they used to bring up on the railway just behind their trenches at Ypres. You could almost set your clock by him, and although our spotter planes were up over the front lines they never seemed to catch him.

There were lots of dog fights (as we called them) overhead with our planes and the Jerries. We watched them most days - about five or six of our planes and the same number of Jerries, sorting each other out, weaving and diving with the rat-a-tat-tat of machine-gun fire. First a Jerry would go down in flames, and then one of our planes, then two more would break off crippled, and try to make it back to base; but I am sure our lads got the better of them every time, because they were always the last to leave the fight.

As the weeks went by we were getting used to the screaming of shells going overhead to Poperinghe, some of them dropping a bit short onto our wagon lines, when, of course, we had to dive for it. As we found out later, in bombardments from enemy shell fire, you would dive down anywhere to avoid the blast of a shell, whether it was in the mud or headlong into a shell hole (like the ostrich who buried its head in the sand). It is no exaggeration to say that we were prepared to dodge behind a small bush or a clump of grass to try and save ourselves when we came under direct machine-gun fire from the Jerry, as I experienced on more than one occasion.

However, to get back to the wagon lines, where I was a very keen soldier, ever anxious to get up to the gun positions at the front. I was soon picked out as a reliable man to go up to the battery positions with the daily rations and ammunitions for the guns. The main idea was that you were a spare man in case any of the drivers got knocked out. Although I was a gunner, I had been given a little training with the horses. So my turn came along to go up to the front line and get my first baptism of gun fire.

The road up to Ypres from Poperinghe was as straight as a die, although very narrow, with the centre of the road made of sets or small blocks of stone which put a camber on the road with just enough room for two vehicles to pass each other. If you got pushed off the centre with your gun limbers you were in the ditch which ran along each side of the road. Then there were the shell holes we had to dodge, plus the shells which were screaming over our heads and at times dropping on our convoys; and also the Infantry who walked along single file going up as reinforcements to the Manchester lads and the Staffordshire lads, who held part of the line on the Ypres front.

It made one feel sick, ready to vomit, as legs and arms went up in the air when Jerry dropped one amongst us, but it was a case of 'an eye for an eye and a tooth for a tooth', as the saying goes. Both sides used to range their guns on each other's main supply roads leading up to the front lines during the daytime; then at night time, all they had to do, knowing they had got the correct range, was to shell the main roads anytime, intermittently, and they were bound to get some of us.

This was my first time up to the front line although I had already experienced the horrors of war. Our convoy, like all other vehicles, was halted at Vlamertinghe, a little village on the main road about $1\frac{1}{2}$ miles from the town of Ypres. No vehicles were allowed beyond this point until after dusk, because the road just beyond the village was under full observation of Jerry's sausage balloons. There was an MP and armed guard at the spot to see that the orders were carried out but Infantry were allowed through in single file with a space of so many yards between each man.

We could hear the rumble of the German convoys on the cobbled roads on their side of the front line, although it would be about two miles away as the crow flies, and when we got the all clear I suppose they could hear our convoys. And now, up the Ypres road and through the Menin Gate into the town of Ypres. As we entered the town and went through the square we passed a huge statue of our Blessed Lord on a massive cross. They used to call him the Old Man of Ypres. The town had been very battered at that time, November 1915. On the right in the square you could see the half demolished houses with little shelves on the bedroom walls still carrying small statues of our Blessed Lady and our Blessed Lord, seeming still to defy the German shelling. On the left, going towards the battle front, stood Clothe Hall, or half of it to be precise, as this had had a battering like the remainder of the town; then to Hell Fire Corner (rightly named) - I think the Germans had about half their artillery trained on that spot.

We turned left at Hell Fire Corner and up through the ramparts to Zillebeke, which was our gun position, just in front of a sunken road that enabled us to proceed to the battery under a certain amount of cover.

During the unloading of stores and ammunition I made acquaintances with some gunners and NCOs. Up to that time we had been complete strangers, but it is amazing how soon one gets on together under conditions like these. By the time we had unloaded our delivery, the gunners had brewed up a good dixie of tea, and they left us to it while they went to the Sergeants' dug-out to collect the mail. This was sent up on the convoy from the wagon lines, and was the most important item of the day, as far as they were concerned. When we had drunk up, the drivers got mounted and we shouted cheerio to the gunners and were on our way back to Poperinghe - a lot faster than we had come up.

It was trotting and galloping most of the way back, but we only got as far as Hell Fire Corner before we were pulled up with a jerk. A gun team had been practically wiped out on the corner by a German 5.9, which was Jerry's most devastating gun of the War. Infantry and stretcher bearers were dragging two of the drivers away, both of whom were dead, with arms and legs missing, plus three horses which had been killed outright. The team belonged to the 42nd Division, which had just moved up to the sector.

As soon as the infantry men had moved the limbers and trucks away, we were able to get through, on our way back to Poperinghe at a good trot. If any shells came over we would not have known anything about them unless they hit us because the noise of the horses and the heavy army vehicles on the cobbled roads drowned out the screaming shells. We arrived back at the wagon lines all in one piece. We gave the drivers a hand to feed and water the horses and tether them up to the lines, before we went back to the bug house. Another day gone.

Each of the new lads got a turn to go up to the front line with stores

Ammunition limbers going to the front.

The Menin road.

every evening, and most of them who got their first dose of shell fire with both sides shelling throughout the night on strategic roads intermittently, knowing they were bound to hit some convoy or other. I can only say how fortunate we were on most of our trips up to the front line.

Our days were taken up with the usual fatigues. Drivers had to clean and groom the horses and the gunners had to wash and clean the limbers, and when that was done, any time left was detailed to help the drivers to clean the harness. After being there for about four weeks we were detailed off for a bath parade. It was all 'detail' in the army. Our journey was to take us to the little town of Poperinghe to a disused slaughter house with three or four of the old round and shallow tubs used to scald and scrape the slaughtered pigs. The tubs were about five or six feet in diameter and about 1½ to 2 feet deep, and God knows how many infantry had already been in that tub of water (or more correctly sludge) - I would say at least a battalion; it was so thick you couldn't possibly fall down; you could cut it with a knife. After trying to wash in that lot we queued up for a clean change of clothes, which were a damn sight lousier than the ones we had just handed in!

As we went along we began to realise that despite the War, with all its shortcomings and gimmicks, most of the lads had a good sense of humour. I well remember one night about this time. It was my turn to go up to the gun position with the rations and mail, and as I stated earlier, the convoy was always halted at the cross-roads at Vlamertinghe until after dusk. Just over the crossing was a soup kitchen, dug out of the side of the bank and well protected by sandbags to withhold a direct hit from a medium size shell. It was free for all troops going up to the front line and on the shelf at the side were empty pork and bean tins. All you had to do was grab an empty tin and rush into the dug out (no loitering) where a couple of infantry men stood behind two huge boilers, one with hot soup in and the other containing boiling water, so you could have soup or tea, whichever you preferred.

The tins were all mixed up. Some were empty, and some already had tea and sugar in. I jumped back upon the limber, when the MP gave us the all clear. I had had a ladle of hot soup put into my tin and you had to sip it slowly out of the tin, not being in possession of knife, fork and spoon when 'dining out' like this. As I got lower down the tin, I found it sweeter and sweeter until it began to make me heave. I said to one of the drivers when we came to a halt, "By gad, that soup is pretty sweet they make down at that soup kitchen". "I know what you have done, you daft bugger," he said, "you must have grabbed a tin with tea and sugar in!"

As I said before, you learn as you go along. We got back safely again that night. A few days later it was the turn of me and another gunner to be sent up to the battery position as reinforcements for two gunners who had been knocked out. I reported to my No 1 in 'A' subsection. He was, of course, a Sergeant, but I thought I had joined the 'Bantams'. He was only 5ft and a bit, when all gunners had to be 5ft. 9ins! Below that you had to be a driver. Nevertheless he was a grand little fellow; his name was Sanders and he was a Cockney, and I got on very well with him, as you will notice in my later chapters.

I had not been up at the front line very many days before Jerry launched a heavy attack on our section of the front. It was a gas attack with mustard gas and we had a great number of casualties through burns.

The road to Ypres.

A gas attack at Ypres.

Chapter 4
From Ypres to Armentières

It was the first time I had seen a gas attack. It was early in December 1915. Our respirators were really old fashioned; although our government had not overlooked the possibility that the Germans would at some time try it. Our respirators were made like a hood, similar to those worn by the Ku Klux Klan. They had two circular eye-pieces let in, and a rubber tube with a mouth-piece leading from the inside through the material, which appeared to be made of flannelette, to the outside, where the rubber tube was flattened to enable the wearer to breath outwards, but would not allow air to be breathed in. The entire hood, which was saturated with a chemical liquid, had to be pulled over your head and tucked into your tunic around the neck.

Believe me, if you were not gassed within half an hour of putting it on by the stench of the chemicals it was saturated with, you were lucky, so you had to take it off and get gassed or leave it on and get gassed. To make matters worse, during the same period the glass eyelets would all get steamed up inside due to the heat from your body. We had a lot of casualties from burns as well as from the other shelling. The gas shells seemed to be small ones - about 2 inches in diameter - and the gas coming from them seemed to be heavier than air, hanging low over the surface of the ground and seeping down into the dugouts. Scores of infantry came down past our guns with their eyes and faces bandaged up, probably blinded for life. Although Jerry had picked his time for the attack, there was a change of wind in the night and he got some of it back on his own trenches.

To the left of our section of the line stood Hill 60, and between that and our gun positions (Zillebeke), stood a piece of high ground we called the Bluff. This ground had been taken and lost and then retaken several times, and now, as we were 'A' Subsection and right of the line, we were detailed off to go on a mission as a forward gun to be taken right up into the support trenches in the night, to blast Jerry off the high ground for good. It was dotted all over with miniature 'pill boxes' or little concrete dugouts, just to hold a machine gunner, and they played havoc with our lads who were sent out on night raids to try to collect a prisoner for interrogation.

A gang of 'pioneers' had been working for a few days on a sunken road, making a temporary track up to the support trenches from a little village called Dickebusche to our place of action, which was the remains of another little village by the name of Voormezeele, just behind St Elo, where the 46th

Division were (The North Midland).

When the pioneers had got the rough road ready we drew our gun out of Zillebeke and came down to the Ypres road to Vlamertinghe and turned left along the Dickebusche road and left again towards Voormezeele to the support trenches. It was nearing midnight by now and the drivers could not get nearer than about 20 yards from the trenches, so we had to man-handle the guns the last few yards into the position cut in the trench, and then we all set together to chock up the wheels and dig in the 'trail eye', ready for action. The O.P. officer had already worked out the range, which was about 400 yards and as our gunners would say, practically 'open sights'. The zero hour was exactly 4.00am, which was arranged between our C.O. and the Liaison Officer of the Infantry.

We commenced firing spot on and the arrangement was to sweep about one degree each time. The order was 'gun fire', which meant continuous fire until we were ordered to stop. We had extra men in the gun team so that there was no waiting for shells, and we kept that up until we could not open the breach to get another shell up, because of the heat caused by continuous firing. Then our C.O. phoned to the infantry officer and the lads went over the top.

During that hour it was like hell let loose. The Germans sent up their S.O.S. rockets for support from their artillery and Jerry plastered us with shells and machine gun fire. I believe they had an electronic device in use at that time, which could determine the approximate distance of a battery by the flash of its gun. But he did not find our gun, although he had one or two near misses. Our chief casualties were from machine gun fire. We had two drivers and a gunner wounded. As we pulled out and galloped off back to Dickebusche, Sergeant Sanders took the lead horses and I took the centre horses, which was the easiest position of the six-horse team, and we got back to our position in Zillebeke just before daylight. The Manchester lads took the Bluff and never lost it again until our great retreat in 1918. A few weeks later Sergeant Sanders was awarded the D.C.M. for carrying out the mission.

We had just about got back when the Jerries opened up on our sector and gave us a real pasting for a couple of hours. I suppose it was a little retaliation, or maybe he thought we were about to mount a major attack after the little skirmish on our right. Being the last replacement up at the gun position I was detailed, along with another gunner, to take the limber and team back to the wagon lines at Poperinghe and we managed to get through Ypres unscathed, right to the cross-roads at Vlamertinghe just at daylight.

British tank.

British observation balloon descending after a morning's observation above Ypres.

French field kitchen.

The horse lines in a British camp, northern France.

We passed lots of casualties on the way back, chiefly infantry, who were allowed up the road in single file with a fair distance between each man. As most people know, it was the poor old infantry who caught most of the shelling, because when you got a strafing like the ones we had at Ypres, you could not get away without casualties. When we got back to the wagon lines we learnt that we had four casualties up at the battery, a sergeant and three gunners. I, for one, was glad to be away from it for a few hours shut-eye before we were to return up to the front line that evening.

There is always a bit of a lull after each side has done some strafing of each other, but the Ypres front was never quite without its strategic shelling of main roads and cross-roads by both sides, to try to stop transport and reinforcements coming up to the front line. We returned to the battery position all in one piece that night, with a sergeant and three new gunners to replace the casualties, and we found that Jerry had knocked our dugout about a bit with his 5.9in. shells. Athough we had sandbags about four feet deep on the top these would not stop those 5.9s from blowing us up.

Life went on day in and day out under those appalling conditions and it was coming up to Christmas 1915. Believe it or not, when Christmas did arrive both sides seemed to understand what day it was and there was definitely a lull in the shelling from both sides. Well, Christmas came and went and we did not get any turkey or plum pudding but we did get a full ration that day ('half a loaf and a dip in the fat!'). It was really difficult to tell what day of the week it was because we did not have any church parades up at the front, which would have given us a clue that it was Sunday.

The shelling went on day and night, which was a feature on the Ypres front, neither side giving each other any rest, and of course we had our casualties, the same as other units on that part of the line, as it was a real 'hot bed' all through the War, when men you had only known a few days were being blown to oblivion in the air and you could not tell the difference between arms and legs or clods of earth going up sky high. It was something you could not get used to; although some of the brave ones said that if your name is not on it you won't get it, I'll wager that at least 98% of the troops out there had the fear of their name being on it. I for one was one of those 98% and that is something you have got to try and keep down inside yourself or you have had it. In my later chapters, in the big offensives like the Battle of the Somme and the great Battle of Passchendaele, I have said my prayers on more occasions than once and I am not ashamed to admit it.

As we battled on through the winter months of 1915 and towards February and March 1916, rumours began to get around that we were to be withdrawn from the line to have a fortnight's rest, and early in March we were taken behind the lines. Our Division, and the 17th and 42nd Division, were to be relieved by the 6th and 7th Divisions. We went back to a small place by the name of Hazebrouck, which was about 20 miles from the front line and well out of range of Jerry's guns. Apart from the fact that we felt pretty safe back there, it was at first really hard work. The orders soon went around that the following week we were to be inspected by none other than General Rawlinson. Talk about work - spit and polish, everyone and everything had got to be spick and span. Gunners were to wash and polish the limbers, and the drivers were to put a shine on the horses' coats, plus the soaping of saddles and harnesses and the polishing and burnishing of all the steel chains on the traces, which were in a very bad state with rust after four or five months in action.

We all buckled to, each subsection trying to outshine the other with the harnesses, etc. One redeeming thing was that we were to have a pay parade, which enabled us to go into the little town of Hazebrouck for a bottle of vin blanc and still get back to the camp and have a good sleep without the fear of being blown up. Army rules and regulations never let up though; it was still lights out at 22.00hrs and our trumpeter could be heard from miles away - but who cares? - there were very few of us who found our way back to the camp before midnight. As they could not afford to put a guard around all the hedgerows of the camp and a lot of us had had a good bit of training in PT, it was a piece of cake, as the saying goes.

It was a hard slog up to the great day before the Big Brass was coming to inspect us. Like all generals, he was over an hour late in arriving. Both the horses and the troops were glad when it was all over, which did not take more than half an hour. He commended the officers and NCOs on our smart turnout. After that it was plain sailing. With everyone all cleaned up we had nothing to do after roll call in the morning, only help the drivers to water and feed the horses, so for our last week behind the lines we had it pretty cushy and were able to go down to the Estaminet for a drink each evening, as long as the francs lasted out. The end of the week soon came along and it leaked out that we were moving to another part of the line, which turned out to be Armentières, on the right of Neuve Eglise, which was held by the 46th Division (North Midland Division), and was about 20 miles from Ypres. We left Hazebrouck at the weekend.

The drivers took the limbers and our blankets, etc, and we, the gunners, went on the old London omnibus double deckers with solid rubber tyres, passing through small villages like Strazeele, Mevris and Nieppe and onto

'Fox holes'.

18-pounder gun.

Armentières. How we stayed on those French cobbled roads with the old double deckers and the solid rubber tyres, sometimes at an angle of about 45 degrees, I will never know.

When each division had a change over we did not take the guns out of action, but took over our new position with their guns, unless there was a general advance, in which case you took the guns with you that you were in possession of, as you would do if you were moving fresh into action, which only happened to me in battles like the Somme and the Battle of Passchendaele. Unless, this is, that you were detailed off for a forward position. It happened to me in both divisions, the 17th Division and the 48th Division; it always seemed to be my luck to be picked out on a forward gun position - then you had to move it all into the new position.

We arrived in Armentières and were allowed up to the gun position in single file, with a hundred yard sprint just over the railway crossing at the right of the station, which was under close observation by Jerry's 'sausage balloons' - a fact I was to find out very clearly a couple of weeks later. Our new gun position was in a row of battered houses just in front and to the right of Plugge Street Asylum, whose clock tower had almost been demolished by Jerry - no doubt he knew we were using it as an observation post for our artillery. In most cases, when a new C.O. moves into a new position the first thing he wants to do is to confirm that the range of our guns covers the strategic targets of enemy roads, etc, with the result that, after a few rounds from our battery, Jerry naturally tries to sort us out a bit and we are bound to get casualties. We found out that Jerry was no mug, and would not take anything laying down; and so the War went on, knocking each other about.

I was beginning to feel like an old soldier now, plus the fact that I was now Sergeant Sanders' blue eyed boy. He had taken a real liking to me and I was now to be his errand boy down to Armentières, scrounging for French bread or anything that was available, I forgot to add that our gun was in the remains of what used to be the butcher's shop in the row, with the barrel pointing through what was left of the window frame, and well camouflaged.

Back to the sergeant again and my scrounging for him. He was a crafty little so and so. At that time he knew the French franc had been devalued, owing to the state of the War and debts. I think the rate of exchange about that time was almost 30 francs to the £1, and lots of the lads were receiving postal orders in their letters from home, and Sergeant Sanders conceived the idea of changing them for the lads, giving them penny for penny in French coins such as 24 pennies for a two bob piece and 30 pennies for a half crown, with the result he was making almost 5 bob out of every 30 bob's worth of

London double decker
buses transporting
soldiers.

Tracer shells.

49

postal orders, and I was the guy who took the postal orders down into Armentières to get them changed into French francs.

It was when I was returning from one of these journeys that I met the only man I ever knew from home throughout the War. He was a man from Silverdale and his name was Harry Woodcock. He was a baker in Civvy Street, and I am sure that I could recognise him coming down the cobbled road a good half a mile away because he was over six feet tall and had a peculiar walk - he was knock-kneed (I hope if he ever reads my book he will not take offence at the way I have described him). The nearer he came towards me, the more certain I was about his identity, and we met just at the danger spot near the cross-roads. We had just got time to express our greetings to each other, when they were cut short within one minute by several 'whiz bangs' which caused us to dive for cover.

I never saw him again until well after the War was over, although I enquired all over the Potteries. Eventually I tracked him down at Normacot, owing to a letter I sent to the Editor of the Staffordshire Sentinel about 'Mademoiselle from Armentières', whom I met on several occasions at the café near the station where I used to go to have my postal orders changed into francs for the Sergeant. She was no Mademoiselle, she was a Madame - and a very nice looking Madame too, as one writer puts it, and I quote. *"It's odd to think that this was the last woman's face those to die saw, serving beer in the Café de la Paix; and from the café they turned left at the station and then left again for the front line and two miles later they were with their 'maker'."*

The soldier who wrote the song (actually it was a sergeant in the Service Corps), was named Edward Rowland. He died in 1955 at Sutton in Surrey, and the lady's name who gave the idea for writing the song "Mademoiselle from Armentières" was Madame Marie Lecocq. Her daughter still lives in Armentières. A few years ago I read an account of the life of Madame Marie Lecocq in a local paper, which said that she was the widow of a miller she had married in Armentières just before the War, who was killed serving in the French army at Verdun. I believe that Sergeant Rowlands wrote over 20 verses of the song and our troops used to sing them almost as often as "It's a Long Way to Tipperary" or "Pack up Your Troubles in Your Old Kit Bag", - which was my favourite throughout the War.

And now, back to the battery, where we have had a cushy 3 months on a quiet sector of the front with only four casualties............ but there was much more to come!

A village behind the lines.

Prayers before the Battle of the Somme.

Gunners on the Western Front prepare for the July advance.

Chapter 5
The Battle of the Somme

We moved down to the Somme from Armentières in the middle of June 1916, and took up a position just in front of Bray-sur-Somme, which was a little village from which ran a spot they called 'Happy Valley'. We were on the top of one of the ridges of the valley, with our guns in camouflaged dugouts and with a fairly good view of the communication trenches which ran up to the front line.

Right opposite us, on the other ridge, was a battery of 60-pounders or Long Toms, as the troops used to call them. I think they were ex-naval guns mounted on another gun carriage. They had a terrific long barrel and when they fired they went off with a crack almost ten times as loud as our guns, and they had twice the range.

As is usual in a new position, the officer in charge went forward to the support trenches to pick out a suitable place for an O.P. (observation post), where he could send messages by telephone back to the battery as he worked 'ranges' out for the battery to fire on. We were to do quite a lot during the following weeks, and of course the word had leaked out that we were preparing for something BIG, and it must have been very obvious to Jerry too, because the majority of our artillery was firing two or three times the amount of shells over, and most of us were on the same job, blowing up barbed wire entanglements and Jerry's trenches.

We kept that up from the middle of June, almost twenty four hours a day. Gun teams were taking little rests in turns and as luck would have it we had a little stream running through the bottom of the valley where we could go down and get a canvas bucket of water to have a good wash and shave for a change, instead of having to shave in what was left in your dixie of tea. Which brings me to that fellow, Gunner Campbell, I mentioned in my previous chapter. Gunner Campbell was the cleanest man in the battery. He was the sanitary man for the battery, and had easy access to the chloride of lime which had a dozen and one uses in the battery. He used to soak his underwear in the chloride of lime for about three days, then dig a hole in the field behind the battery and bury his clothes for a week, then dig them up and wash them. Away had gone the lice and all the 'nits' too. The lads of course could always introduce humour into it all by putting the visitors back!

But we must get back to the serious side of the War, where a ceaseless shelling of Jerry's trenches and barbed wire entanglements was kept up until zero hour, which was 07.30am 1st July, 1916, in broad daylight; and the biggest mistake they made throughout the War:

The attack should have been made just as dawn was beginning to break, as the experts now know. Someone behind the lines made the biggest bloomer in the world and cost the British army almost 60,000 casualties in dead and wounded on that first day of the Battle of the Somme. I saw hundreds of our young lads who had only just got their heads above the parapets killed before they could even get out of the trenches. I turned several of them over, thinking that I might be able to recognise some of them, and many of them could have been no more than 17 years of age. To make matters worse the German barbed wire defences we were supposed to have blown to pieces were practically untouched, after we had been strafing them from the middle of June! I actually saw this when we went through with our guns.

The 1st of July 1916 was like hell upon earth, if that was possible. The deafening roar of all sizes and calibre of guns. As a four gun battery of 18 pounders, we were firing 1,000 rounds per day and that was kept up on a front of about 18 miles. On the second day we saw a batch of German prisoners coming down the valley, and as we had got a short lull in our firing I and another gunner ran down the slope to have a look. There were about 50 or 60 of them, the first prisoners we had seen in a large batch.

Jerry was strafing us like hell with his 5.9 inch time shells which were bursting in front of our battery about 50 to 100 feet high. One burst right in front of our gun, and we heard a piece of shrapnel screaming through the air towards our gun. We knew it had hit it; one got used to the noise of shells and shrapnel in their traverse through the air. We clambered back up the slope to our battery and found that a piece of shrapnel had hit one of our Sergeants, named Williams, who had only been back off leave that very day from 'Blighty'. There had been two sergeants standing at the side of our gun pit watching the prisoners down below. They heard the shell coming, and Sergeant Dillon dived to the right and Sergeant Williams dived to the side of the gun pit straight in the path of it. They were just spreading a blanket to put him in when we arrived at the top. The piece of shrapnel had split him right down the middle as a butcher would split open a sheep's carcass.

This was the first of many casualties our battery was to suffer on the Somme. As I told you previously, our battery was situated on one side of the ridge in Happy Valley and we had a clear view of our support trenches. When

Haig and Joffre, 1st July 1916.

Ready to go over the top, 1st July 1916.

the first big mine was blown up a minute or so before 07.30hrs, we saw it clearly, a huge hump forcing itself skyward and spreading out like a gigantic mushroom, up to 200-300 feet high and about 10 seconds later the ground shook under our feet. We heard later that one of the several mines which were to be blown up was delayed by some technical fault and went up among some of our infantry men, causing a lot of casualties, burying them under huge boulders of chalk and earth.

As another eyewitness said, *"the waves of infantry men kept moving forward and being mowed down like rows of wheat"*, wave after wave caught by the German machine gunners who had come up out of their dugouts after our barrage had lifted beyond their trenches. Our lads were caught and mowed down on Jerry's wire which was an obstacle we thought had been cleared away, and they were sitting ducks for the German machine gunners. There were so many of our lads trying to go forward across no man's land, they could not miss, and the Germans, who were past masters of concrete with their concrete pill boxes, had sills of concrete on their parapets and firing steps, plus steel shields that could move up or down to protect their machine gunners, all of which we were to learn about later further on at Passchendaele.

Our lads were just mown down and the dead lay as they had fallen and the wounded lay with them or took cover wherever they could, such as a shell hole or behind the body of a dead comrade. If any in the line were missed the German gunners would traverse back with another sweep until they had wiped out almost the whole of the line. In spite of the terrible fire the infantry kept going. The German machine gunners in their miniature pill boxes and their adjustable steel shields were well protected from our rifle fire. The few individual survivors who managed to get through were hung up at the German wire and slaughtered. *"How any of us got through to the German trenches I will never know,"* said one of the Manchester battalion.

We covered the infantry up to the 3rd July as our advance was very slow, owing to the stubborn resistance of the German machine gunners. Progress could be measured in hundreds of yards towards Fricourt and Montaubon. We now pulled our guns out and proceeded towards our new positions right opposite the first of the large mines which our engineers had blown up. We had little difficulty in crossing our old first line trenches, as they had been blown to pieces by the German artillery - it was here that I rolled over one or two of our young lads to have a look if I could recognise any of them.

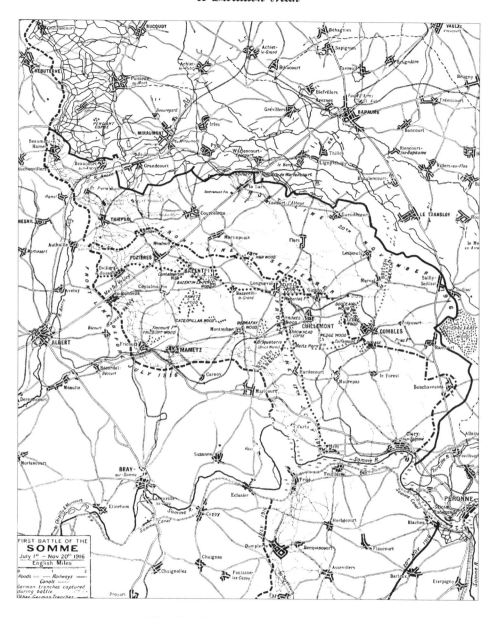

The First Battle of the Somme 1916.

It got worse as our teams with our guns tried to thread our way through the corpses which lay about in the old no man's land - hundreds upon hundreds of our lads lay there as we came into the old German front line. We lived among them for the next few days. During the lull in our firing, I went over to the enormous mine they had blown up on the 1st of July; my chief reason to get myself fixed up with a steel helmet, because it was only the infantry who had been issued with them up to that time, owing to the short supply of them. Which gives the reader some idea of how unprepared we were at the outbreak of the War!

All around the top of the mine, which had left a hole as big as a marl hole, lay dozens of dead infantry lads, so I took what seemed to me a good helmet off one lad but when I rolled him over I found a bullet hole in the front of the helmet and the bullet had gone around and around the inside of the steel hat, tearing out most of the webbing, before it had entered his head. I came to another lad, who had been hit with a piece of shrapnel straight between the eyes which had made a triangle 2in. x 2in. x 2in. and pushed his eyes and nose into the back of his head. I knew the poor lad would not need his steel helmet any more, so I took it.

In the meantime, stretcher-bearers and pioneers were laying the dead in the bottom of a mine hole, like building a house with bricks, a layer one way and a layer crossways, and vice versa. I should say there must have been about 500 as I stood at the top of the mine hole and listened as the Padré read the burial service on that whole heap of death.

Within about ten minutes I returned to my battery over the uneven ground and shell holes, having to duck and dive several times as the Germans were shelling us constantly with 'whiz bangs', a gun which fired a shell of about 50 millimetres, and also his 5.0 which were real block busters. We lost two gunners that day and two more wounded as we had no shelter at all, only shell holes and the old trenches nearby in which to take cover. The only thing which was good for the time being was the weather, which was sunny and hot with a few storms that gradually increased as the days went by, and was to make our position like a quagmire later on.

The word soon got round when they found that I had got a steel helmet. The first chance any of the lads got, they were over to the 'marl hole' searching in the discarded equipment for steel helmets. Soon we were all fixed up. About four or five days later, we limbered up and moved forward towards Fricourt and Mametz Wood. Our troops had already taken Montana, a place I was to have cause to remember later on, and as we went through the

German wire most of it was still intact. Our lads still lay around and across the wire as they had been mowed down by the German machine gunners. We were soon across the Jerries' front line trenches - what was left of them. We had given them a frightful bashing and had levelled them almost to the ground. The dead lay all around. Both the Germans and our lads, more than ever I had seen before. They were all around us. They had been laying out there for ten or eleven days in the hot sun and intermittent rain. They were nearly all black and bloated and ready to burst. Talk about feeling sick, I could have heaved my heart out. Literally scores of them and it was difficult to tell one from the other; only by the colour of their uniform. The stretcher-bearers had been too busy with the wounded to trouble about the dead.

We soon got our guns switched around and ready for action. Our O.C. had gone up in front to pick out an old dugout or some other shelter for an observation post from which to direct our gunfire on the German gun positions or any Jerries who were escaping along the roads. We spoke to a lot of our lads, 'walking cases' who were wounded, as they passed down through our guns, who told us how they had to force their way fighting all through Mametz Wood.

Our artillery were still strafing Guillemont and Ginchy, with the heavies pounding away at Contalmoison and Bazentin. We were at it most of the day once we had registered on our targets and, of course, through the night as well when our infantry sent up an SOS for support. It was a case of getting forty winks when you could, either in an old trench or shell hole, but you could not go to sleep. Jerry was lobbing them over you and around you all night, and most of the time you could not get the stench of the rotting corpses out of you nostrils; you were almost forced to put your gas mask on. We were in a cemetery without any headstones and we had to wait until night fall before we could brew up to make a hot drink.

On the 16th August, an attempt was at length made to carry out the first stage of a pre-arranged scheme. It met, however, with only partial success. A few days later, after a preliminary bombardment lasting thirty-six hours along the whole line of the German trenches and the works from Orvillers to the Somme, a larger combined attack was undertaken. In spite of a number of enemy counter-attacks, the most violent of which, levelled at the point of junction of the British and the French, succeeded in forcing our allies and ourselves back from a part of the ground won, valuable progress was made. Our troops established themselves on the outskirts of Guillemont village and occupied Guillemont Station.

In the meantime, our drivers (God bless them) were up to the gun positions every night just at dusk with their mules as pack horses, carrying ammunitions and stores up to the battery. Each mule was carrying eight 18 pounder shells on a saddle made of canvas sack. The drivers were so cheerful and they conveyed to us any fresh news from the wagon lines. Sometimes it was a gunner's turn to go on leave to Blighty and oh, how I wished I was going with him, but there is a old saying *"It all comes to those who care to wait"*, and my turn was to come sooner than I expected. We had lost all contact with the calendar and each and every day was the same to us. It was action stations intermittently day and night, trying to doze off for a short period during a lull, laying down at the side of the gun. The only thing that changed was the weather, which got worse, and with only an army ground sheet and one blanket I found myself sometimes almost drowned, just as if I had been thrown into a horse trough.

We had our casualties like other units, but we all still held the conviction that if your name was on it you would get it. One got used to the screaming and whining of shells and if you could hear them you were relatively safe because they were on one side of you or the other. But if you never heard the one which was coming your way, you never would. I know that sounds a bit Irish, but it is true, because I know that I have had one or two near misses - and the last one caught me, but I am pleased to say I am still living to tell this story.

If the shell is coming straight at you, you never hear it, but to the side of you, yes. It is pretty obvious with Jerry's whiz bangs, which are a projectile about 2 inches in diameter and have a muzzle velocity of about 2,000 feet per second, which means the bloody thing is with you before you have heard it, as sound only travels at 1,100 ft per second. My gun was a 18 pounder, which fires a shell 3 inches in diameter and has a muzzle velocity of just over 1,600 ft per second, so there were a lot of ours which Jerry could not dodge.

But let us get back to the War again. Reinforcements kept moving up past our guns, and moving in the other direction were the wounded men, both stretcher cases and walking wounded, British and German. Also batches of German prisoners were being escorted back down the line. The rain was terrific and turned the ground into a quagmire. The only safe way to walk was on the duck boards and if you slipped off these you were doomed. The German bombardment had increased as they retreated on to dryer ground and no matter whether they were wounded or fresh reinforcements, out in the

Heavy Howitzer.

Field surgery.

open, when the shells dropped in amongst them, the arms and legs went flying into the air like clumps of grass.

On the 20th July, we had orders to pull out and advance almost two miles to a ridge of high ground overlooking the little village of Montana, passing Mametz Wood and overlooking Delville Wood and Longueval.

In all the accounts that I have read about the Great War, there is no mention of any attempt at a cavalry charge, but I know there was such an attempt, because when our troops took Montana they tried a break through with a cavalry charge. I saw dozens of cavalry horses lying dead on the ridge overlooking Montana. We drove our guns right through them and they were not gun team horses. They must have been lying out there for more than two weeks and were almost ready to burst. The stench was awful.

We went into action on the ridge that night, and as our C.O. had got a rough sketch of the German trenches on his map, he concentrated on the Jerry front line for that night. Where there is a ridge there is always a sunken road. During a lull in the firing we managed to dig a fox hole in the side of the bank for a rest. The word had gone around that we were preparing for another major attack on Jerry. It was the 22nd July, and a violent counter-attack on Guillemont Station was repulsed. On the next day further important progress was made on a wide front, north and east of Delville Wood (or Devil's Wood, as the lads called it).

The bombardment which preceded and accompanied these operations was, in actual fact, a work of absolute annihilation of every German at whom it was directed. Observers were unanimous in concluding that it was unprecedented in the history of warfare. This attack kept us busy for the next 24 hours and towards the middle of the day, 23rd July, it eased off a bit and we managed in turns to 'brew up' or heat up a dixie of soup and get a little rest.

We were looking forward to a quieter night and I was lying in my fox hole, having a smoke after a good brew of tea, thinking of home and lots of other things, when the Sergeant blew his whistle for action stations. It was about 22.00hrs and our infantry had sent up an SOS with the familiar red and green rockets. We rushed up the ridge, and were in action before you could say 'Jack Robinson', to give them support, for the Germans were bashing hell out of our trenches and may have been making a night attack.

As there are several men in each gun team who can lay the gun, the first one there gets in the No. 3 seat ready to take the orders. I finished up as No 5, handing the shells up for loading, and we were firing as fast as No 4 could

The battle area and trenches of Longueval and Delville Wood - 'Devil's Wood'.

slam them up the breech. But the Jerries had noticed our gun flashes and it was not long before he began to lob 5.9s at us, hitting left and right with time busting shells. One landed just above our gun and in front.

I had just passed another shell into the hands of No 4, and as I turned around it hit me and spun me around and down I went. Lieutenant Smith was standing quite close to me and picked me up and as he saw the blood pouring out of my arm. He tore his own field dressing off and tied me up and just said *"Heraty, down to the casualty clearing station, you'll find it, just follow the others."*

Threading our way down the ridge, we walked past those old dead cavalry horses, dodging Jerry's shells until we reached the C.C.S., where we were soon given first aid and loaded into ambulances. Soon we were out of range of Jerry's guns. They drove us to Rouen on the River Seine and we sailed right through from Rouen to Southampton on the new hospital ship, the St Andrew (which, incidentally was the first hospital ship to be commissioned in the Second World War).

We landed at Southampton and the Red Cross train was already waiting in the docks, along with several others. Ambulance men and nurses were as busy as ants, unloading stretcher cases off the ship and onto the trains. It was a doddle for me, I was only a walking case and no one felt better than me to know that I was out of that hell hole over in France for a while. The attendants on the train could not do enough for us, tea and sandwiches and also cigarettes. When we tasted good old English bread again, we knew we were in Blighty. It was still dark as the train moved out of the docks, as they had timed the crossing over the 'Herring Pond' (or English Channel) to coincide with the darkness, because the Germans did not differentiate between a cargo ship or a hospital ship if it came within striking distance of their submarines.

We were on our way to hospital, which turned out to be the 3rd Western General Hospital at Newport in Monmouthshire, which to locals was the Snow Hill Hospital. This was to be our residence for the next three months. After a few weeks the wounded who could walk were allowed out into the town. The people of Newport were wonderful in every way, and treated us all as if we had each won a V.C. Everything was free for the wounded Tommies; picture houses, fêtes, free rides on the trams, the lot. But army rules still held fast, even in hospital, for it was still 'lights out' at 22.00 hours. The lads had always got means and ways, such as asking a civilian who happened to be passing by to give them a leg over the wall. We could also get into one of the

The wounded on the dockside.

Ferrying the wounded to the hospital ship.

No. _____
(If rep__ __,
above

N. _____ Record Office,

_____ Woolwich _____ Station.

___ 14th August ___, 1916.

Sir,

I regret t__ __ve to inform you that a report has this day been received from the War Office to the effect that (No.) _107274_

(Rank) _Gunner_ (Name) _A. J. Heraty_

*Strike out words that do not apply.

(Regiment) _Royal Field Artillery_ was { *dangerously* *severely* *slightly* }

wounded in action at _place not stated admitted to_
5 General Hospital Rouen
on the _24th_ day of _July_ 1916.
Gun wound

I am at the same time to express the sympathy and regret of the Army Council.

Any further information received in this office as to his condition will be at once notified to you.

I am,

Sir,

Your obedient Servant,

COLONEL
R.   & R.F.A. RECORDS.
Officer in charge of Records.

Mr. A. Heraty

Mr Heraty
15 Bailey St

The contents and outside of the letter my parents received regarding my first injury.

corridors from the outside loo, thus dodging the guard on the entrance gate.

The time in hospital seemed to fly by and after weeks of sight-seeing around the town and being taken to Tredegar Park on several occasions, the days rolled on to Christmas 1916. We would soon be discharged from hospital to go on ten days' leave and then out to France again. Towards the end of November 1916, they lined up about 20 or 30 of us outside the hospital. We were to be finally checked out by the Surgeon, who was a Captain in the R.A.M.C. He came along the line, asking each man how he was, and did he feel fit enough to go on sick leave, and then after that to join his unit. They all seemed ready to go - so they could all be at home sweet home for ten full days. At last the officer arrived to my turn in the line and said, *"Well, Heraty, do you feel fit enough to go on sick leave?"*.

"Well, Sir," I replied, *"the pain in my arm is so acute I cannot lift my arm up right."*

"Let me have a look at your wound, and your arm. Where do you feel the pain?" he asked, as he felt my arm.

I said *"Between my wrist and my elbow."*

He pressed it in various places, looked at my wound, and said *"The wound seems to have healed up nicely."* Then he suddenly said *"Heraty, you will have to go back into hospital and the Sister will come around to see you in about 15 minutes."*

I went back into my ward and sat on the bed until the Sister came along to see me, and said, *"Heraty, you'd better undress and get back into bed again, you are for the X-ray theatre."* They took me along in a wheelchair, and in about 20 minutes they brought me back again and the Sister said, *"You just sit on your bed for about half an hour and I will be back to see you."* She was dead on time, and said *"Heraty, get back into bed again, you are for the operating theatre. They will be along for you in about ten minutes."*

They were along in due course and they wheeled me on a stretcher along to the operating theatre. They strapped me down on the table and I well remember the Doctor saying, *"Now young fellow you must start counting, nice and slowly until I tell you to stop."*

I recall counting up to 24 but I never heard him say stop. But one thing I do know, when I came around about five hours later, I was back in my old bed in the ward and he must have spilled half the chloroform down my neck instead of on the pad which they put over your nose and mouth in those old fashioned days, and it burnt all down my neck; but I was glad to be awake again. About half an hour later, the Sister came along and put a small X-ray photograph on my locker and also a small shrapnel bullet, $^3/_4$ of an inch in diameter. *"These are yours, Heraty. Souvenirs."* she said.

The shrapnel bullet had entered at the base of my thumb where it joins the top of the palm of my hand and travelled right up my wrist into my arm. They had healed the wound at the base of the thumb but they did not know that the shrapnel bullet was still in my arm. To cut a long story short, when I was fit enough to go out again, they took us for a trip round Tredegar Park again. I used to keep the bullet in the top pocket of my hospital blues and must have been romping in the park and lost it out of my pocket. I was a bit disappointed at losing my souvenir. It had enabled me to get back to Blighty, and I managed to get home for Christmas, which was wonderful for me. But you can imagine my ten days' leave flew by quicker than a shell.

Ironically, I got my warrant to report back to the same barracks from where I had originally started out in my training - the Northumberland Fusiliers Barracks at Newcastle-upon-Tyne. We were treated like Old Sweats, of course, and the 'Rookies' looked upon us as Old Soldiers too, and wanted us to tell them what it was like, over there in France. They had not long to wait. Although it was only the middle of January 1917, they were soon on draft along with us to go over to France on active service.

So we were on our way again to another tour of duty over in France, but this time there were quite a lot of us with previous experience who knew 'how many beans made five'. The procedure was much the same as it was in 1915, but we had a few days' stay at a transit camp in a place called Hemel Hempstead, near London,. It was here that they sorted us out to our different units and where these were to be sent as reinforcements.

Our first stop was, of course, the docks at Southampton and then on board another tramp steamer and across the Channel to Le Havre. From the dock over in France we were sent about four miles up the coast to a small town called Harfleur, to another transit camp which was composed chiefly of bell tents.

I shall always remember this camp, because that year, 1917, we had one of the most severe winters I have experienced. It was three months of continual frost, and we were in bell tents, 30 men to each tent, with all our equipment, when the usual complement was only 12 men per tent. We all had to get down together and all up together, like sardines in a tin. There was a song going around about that time which the older ones like me well remember and really fitted ("The more we are together, together, etc").

We were only at this camp for about ten days when we were loaded into cattle trucks again to be sent up to the front line, but during that time we had a pay day at that camp, and I well remember my pay for a week was 5 francs. One could hardly set the town alight on that. But we did manage to see a little more of the French way of life during our short stay at the camp. Although we had been out to France before, previously we were rushed up straight to the battle front to stem the tide of the German onslaught at the time. At that camp we got our first session of Housey Housey, which they now call Bingo, and Woodbines were 10½d for a tin of 50.

There was an old time-serving soldier in our tent who had been out in 1914, and this was his second time out, and believe me, he knew all the answers. He was a Welshman and naturally they all called him Taffy. As he knew the ropes he took three or four of us to what he called the Bull Ring at Le Havre. (Did I say I was as green as grass, early in my story? I must have been joking, I was a real cabbage). We walked down to Le Havre from Harfleur, which was about four miles, to save the four centimes tram fare, and I was all eyes, looking for a big arena, and all excited, thinking that I was going to see a bull fight. We called in one or two estaminets on the way down for a glass of beer, which was 1d a glass at that time. It would be just under half a pint, probably ¼ litre, and then on our way again, and still I was all eyes, so I said to Taffy, *"When are we coming to the big arena?"*. He said *"You'll see a bit lower down"*, and so we did.

He took us along the quayside, down a road called the Rue de Gallion and into a large estaminet, which was crowded with soldiers and sailors of all nationalities. There were about a dozen young women with nothing on, only a smile. I could have dropped my 'cabbage'! I did not know such places existed, but you learn. We managed to weather the storm for the evening and made our way back to the camp with very little of the 5 Francs we had started out with. Eventually, when we got back, Taffy told me that this road was called the bull ring, and the place he had taken us to was called 'The House with the Red Lamp'.

The days soon rolled by and we were on our way in a cattle truck as reinforcements to join our new Division, which was the 48th Division (South Midlands). The 48th Division was in action at a place called 'Herbecourt'. Guess where? The Somme of course.

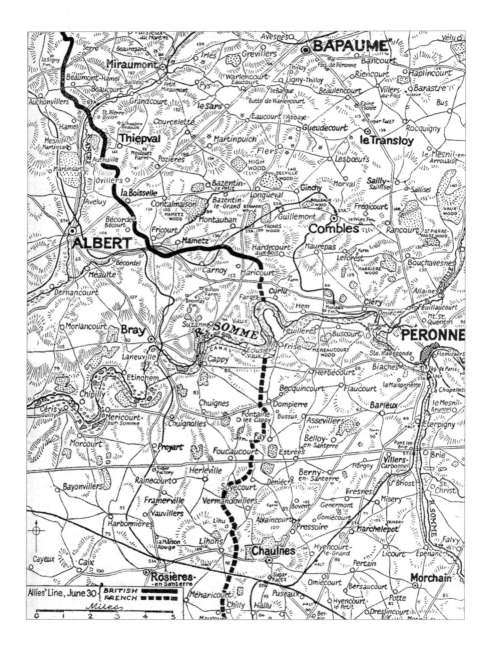

Chapter 6
The Evacuation of Peronne

After spending a couple of days and nights in the cattle trucks and being shunted onto the side lines at Amiens and Albert, we were landed at a little village by the name of Cappy, where the wagon lines of our Brigade (24-48th Division) were stationed. Our guns were in action at a place called Herbicourt, two to three miles further up the line, on territory we had captured from the Germans during the Somme Battle. Happy Valley, the area immediately in front of Bray-sur-Somme and looking towards Mametz Wood had been my position when the battle started in 1916. The ground on which we now found ourselves contained a lot of old German dugouts. Our lads had cleaned them out a bit and they were being used by part of our battery for sleeping accommodation and, for other purposes as well, which I will explain as my story goes along, especially about the stratagem of the cooks.

The majority of the battery were billeted in an old farmyard, similar to the one we were in at Poperinghe, just behind Ypres. The officers and the NCOs were billeted in what remained of the old farmhouse, and the troops had the hard floor of the old barn with bits of straw scattered over it. That was your bed, and believe me it did not take us long to get ready for bed, because we got down as we got up, not being able to take our gun boots off for days on end because if you did, well, you would not be able to get them on again without thawing them out on a some lighted straw.

It was now January 1917, and we had already been frozen up for about six weeks with more to come. This was Cappy, where the broken up old track was potted with shell holes and the GS wagons had to negotiate them to bring up our rations. Many times the wagons used to get stuck in the shell holes and tip over into the mud, water and ice. By the time supplies reached our battery the food was frozen up like lumps of clay, but we had to put up with what we got. We did not get much bread. Sometimes it worked out at about 30 men to one loaf of bread, so it was chiefly bully and biscuits for days on end.

We were new reinforcements to this 48th Division, and we had to stay at the wagon lines and help the drivers with the horses, watering and feeding them and trying to clear the caked-on mud off them. Talk about mud. Of course we were still on the Somme and it all looked the same in ordinary times, but because the ground was all frozen up it appeared solid - until you stepped off the duck boards. Hell Fire! - down you would sink almost to your

Peronne

Arras

waist. It used to take around twenty minutes to walk about twenty yards to fall in for Roll Call. This was Cappy!

As I mentioned there was thirty to a loaf of bread, but it got a bit better later on, when we sometimes used to get four to a loaf, even if it was frozen as hard as a bullet and the old bill hook used to come in very handy for splitting it up! Even then it was a case of tossing a coin up as to see who should get the bread. As most Old Soldiers know, the army turned us into a lot of scroungers. To quote an old saying *'a full belly never falls for a empty one'*, and if you were to report anything missing to your Sergeant or another NCO, they would say, *"You know what to do - pinch somebody else's"*.

Which brings me back to the old dugout I mentioned. The cooks drew the rations from the Quarter Master's Stores for the battery, and used one of the old dugouts as a bed sitter. Owing to the amount of scrounging and borrowing taking place, everyone used the sugar bags as pillows, with the result that when you went down the steps to collect your ladle of tea in your dixie the bloody lice used to be floating on the top of the tea. Just to make the scene a little more gruesome a fellow called Howlett, who was always late in the ration queue, would be spending his spare time sitting at the top of the dugout steps slaughtering rats with his jack knife. They were caught in a French type of rat trap, quite ingenious and easily made, which consisted of a piece of wire netting (which we call chicken netting) rolled up like a piece of stair carpet with a diameter of about 12 inches, with one end blocked in and the other end turned in like a cone, which allowed the rats to get in but not get out again. The hole in the cone was just big enough for the rats to squeeze in, and then the wire netting would stick into them when they tried to get out.

We were at the extreme right of the British battle front, adjoining the French and their famous 75 guns facing Peronne, a town which was to be in our possession in a few weeks to come. We carried out our 'Active Service' in the mud and frost, which was to stay with us until the March of that year, 1917. But as I have said earlier, there was never any let up of the old Army Rules and Regulations; the horses were to be fed and watered before anyone else each morning.

There were days when we had an occasional break from cleaning the mud and shit off the horses, and we would scrounge all the cordite out of the damaged shell cases and put it in a bag and go round to the dugouts which had been in possession of the Germans before the Somme Battle a few months before. The rats had been having a good time feeding on the dead bodies in the old dug outs and trenches, which remained much the same for months, although they had been battered about a lot by our artillery bombardments. We would get as many rifles and ammunitions as we could scrounge and then we would block up all the holes around except for one into which we would stuff as much cordite as we could. After touching it with a match we would cover the hole with a bag and Wooph! It would simply blow them out in all directions. Believe me some of the buggers were as big a rabbits. We enjoyed ourselves this way for an hour or two until the cordite ran out.

Another day my mate and I were standing at the entrance to the old farmhouse, which was what we called our wagon lines, when we saw a plane coming towards one of our sausage balloons about a mile away and maybe about 500ft high. It was a nice day, with a slight westerly wind blowing, and I said to my mate *"that bloody plane is coming to have a go at the sausage balloon"* (which was overlooking the German lines on observation), and sure enough he was.

We were looking directly at the balloon and saw the complete episode from start to finish. The plane seemed to be coming nice and slowly, at a height of about 1,000ft and I am sure he had throttled his engine down as he slowly dropped to about 500ft. He came in on the right hand side of the balloon as we looked at it, and as he turned on his side,going around the front of the balloon; I am sure the plane was a German Albatross. We heard his machine gun dive a couple of short bursts of fire - rat, tat, tat. A second later the balloon burst into flames. The engineers below tried to wind in the balloon but it exploded and became a ball of flames. One of our observers jumped out of the basket and his white parachute opened out as he sailed down to earth. The other jumped out a few seconds later, but the blazing balloon was catching up on him before he got half way down, as he sailed down towards the German lines with the light westerly breeze that was blowing at the time.

Afterwards we learnt the reason for all this activity. It seems he had attacked the majority of our balloons on that front, because we were seeing too much. As the months went by it all fitted in. Before many days we had orders from Divisional Headquarters in the form of an SOS, to move forward immediately as Jerry had done a bunk and evacuated his defence position, leaving only a rear guard to cover his retreat. Through the devious means of wire tapping, his intelligence had acquired the knowledge that we were preparing for a big attack to the north of our defence. As a mere battery unit we did not know at that time, but in the months that followed it turned out to be the great Battle of Passchendaele, and Jerry was preparing to shorten the battle front on his part of the line, which was a salient. The German High Command decided, by retreating at the time, to straighten their line to take out the salient, which would release four or five divisions to strengthen his defences around Ypres and Passchendaele. I believe this was to form the defences later known as the Hindenburg Line.

We were on the move now, chasing the retreating Germans and going over some of the ground we had won and lost during the Somme Battle. Travelling in a northerly direction we crossed over the ground of Foncquevillers, where the 46th Division (North Midland Division) had lost a lot of good men in the early stages of the Somme Battle. We also passed by the old gun positions held for quite a long time at Hertuterne by my present Division, the 48th, and along the main road towards Pozieres and Bapaume. This was dead straight and similar to the road from Poperinghe to Ypres, but minus the poplar trees which ran each side.

The roads - what was left of them - were cobbled, and the familiar ditches lay on each side, where now lay the remains of about six or seven of our tanks, blown to bits, chipped and rusting. They were stuck in the ditches on both sides, where they must have been a real target for the German gunners on the open ground. As we neared Bapaume we turned right and south towards Peronne.

Our advance was slow but sure, with the units of the Bengal Lancers joining in along the road and over what were once ploughed fields. Of course there were intervals between each unit and we had to be ready to go into action immediately, because we never knew when Jerry might turn around and have a go. We were getting on to strange ground now, passing through little villages such as Epee, Tincourt and a place called Etapigmy, where we were halted for a few days of rest, although it was 'action stations' all the time now, and we dug in our guns in a ploughed field right in front of what was left of a small works just near to the village of Tincourt.

The following morning we noticed Jerry had left a sausage balloon with his rear guard units to try to detect our movements. It appeared to be about three to four miles away as the crow flies. One of our sergeants, by the name of Nixon, who was in charge of our subsection, which was B Subsection, said *"Nick, what about having a go at the German sausage balloon in front of us?"* It was at the extreme range of our gun, the 18 pounder. No sooner said than done, he gathered about four or five of the gunners to dig a hole about 2ft deep at the end of the trail end (which was a gunner's term for the rear end of the gun), and this allowed the trail to be sunk lower in the ground to give the gun greater elevation. When that was done the range finder was set at its extreme range and they decided to have a go. The first shot only seemed yards away so the Sergeant said *"Good, give him six of gunfire."*

If we did not actually hit it we forced the Germans to wind him in very quickly. We made a run for it to the dugouts, but only just in time as we had to run about 100yds to take cover. Within about 15 minutes he was strafing our gun position with his 5.9. Although he dug us out a bit, he never managed to hit our guns. Well, of course, we had a few casualties, mostly shrapnel wounds, but none serious!

The next day we drew out of that position near the Sugar Mill at Tincourt and proceeded on our way towards Peronne. After marching and resting for days we were soon nearing the town, which our infantry were attacking with all their strength. Within a couple of days we had pushed Jerry right out of the town and to the other side, which was going to be his new defence line. As he retreated he had used the Russian's scorched earth policy. He had also poisoned all the water and wells in the town, and booby trapped most of the buildings he had failed to destroy, but our lads had given him a real pasting when they eventually caught up with him.

Our troops had now got a firm hold in the town of Peronne and we could dig in to a more settled position for our guns. The roads over the period of the last few weeks had been choc a bloc with troops of all descriptions, even cavalry. Some were moving forward and some had been relieved from the attack to go to the rear for a short rest for a week or so. I should imagine that at that time the British Army must have had about 40 to 50 divisions on the move, backwards and forwards all the time. Our casualties were very light as the Germans were still fighting a rearguard action until we had pushed them beyond Peronne. We were now at the extreme of the British line where it joined the French and their wonderful 75 guns with which they blasted out the Germans at Noyon just below St Quentin. Although suffering heavy losses, they made all their objectives to join us, and in army terms, we 'consolidated our positions'.

The freezing cold weather was still with us in March. In fact we had snow in that month, but it did not deter our engineers from getting a bridgehead over the River Somme and the nearby adjoining canal. The Germans were nearing the point where they must halt to make a stand, and were getting near to what was to become the Hindenburg Line, as we came to know it later. The Germans began to fling their 5.9 shells at us and of course we had casualties in both drivers and gunners at places like Frise and on the outskirts of Peronne, but there was one redeeming feature; our ration wagons were beginning to catch up with us better, after going astray a time or two, and it was now running at four to a loaf instead of being on 'iron rations' for days on end. I hope my readers will forgive me for treating casualties so lightly now, but the fact was, we had become hardened to the conditions, if one could say that was possible. My only excuse is that you can never grow hardened to hunger.

We were now approaching April-May 1917, and the Canadians were battling hard to capture Vimy Ridge, in which we were later to become involved. During this time we were to loose 20% of our Battery in one night and I was wounded for the second time. Whilst we were still at the Gates of Peronne, the powers that be were busy shaping things out for the big battle which was to take place later; Paschendaele. In June 1917, we had orders to pull out from Peronne and go behind the lines for two weeks rest at a place called Doullens, about 15 miles from Amiens.

Canadians exit the trenches after the battle.

We passed through most of the old battle grounds from Peronne; Heputerne, Pozieres, Albert, and Sailly, skirting the old Badaume road and the broken down old tanks and touching Gommecourt and Fonquevillers and down to Doullens to a rest camp, where we did not have to toss up for a portion of bread like we did in Cappy. We got a full ration at the camp, which was 'half a loaf and a dip in the fat', as we say in the army. And now, for a couple of weeks, we were back to the old Army Rules and Regulations, spit and polish with another general parade of kit, horses and harness, etc.

It was a treat to have a good night's sleep with our boots off. At the weekend five of us got a day pass to go into Amiens, where, of course, several of the streets were out of bounds to the troops for various reasons, such as the street with the 'Hob-Nailed Door', outside which always hung a red lamp. We made the best of the day, calling in at several estaminets for a drink and finally having our photographs taken, a copy of which should appear somewhere near here. As always, holidays of any description seem to fly by very quickly. Before we could sort ourselves out properly, and when we were beginning to get used to the luxury of a shave and a decent wash, we were again under orders to return in a northerly direction to the Battle Front.

As regards our destination, well, your guess could be as good as ours, being only of the rank and file. Only the officers were told of our movements until we arrived, but the pattern seemed to unravel itself as we passed through, or near the following places, or what remained of them. As we made our way towards the battle front we turned left, skirting the old No Mans Land of Gommecourt and Arras and passing close to Vimy Ridge and Bethune. We went through the outskirts of Armentiéres and up towards the Ypres front, towards St Julien. We passed close to our old wagon lines near Poperinghe, where I had joined the 17th Division in 1915. I noticed on some of the units which we passed, the Draught Board Division, the 23rd Division, and I was all eyes, looking out, hoping that I might see some signs of my old Division, the 17th.

On the way up we had one or two breaks, putting up at various farm houses and barns with the usual bit of straw for a bed. We finally came to some old shacks opposite the Dicky Bush Road, which were to be our wagon lines for the weeks that followed. Our gun positions were up towards St Julien and Poelcappelle, which lay between the Germans and the Paschendaele Ridge. So now we knew what we were in for!

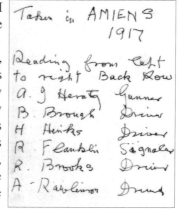

The back of the photograph on the opposite page.

Passchendaele

Chapter 7
The Great Battle of Paschendale

We had now arrived at what we termed our 'wagon lines', which lay between Poperinghe and Ypres. We had no way of knowing that we had been switched from General Rawlingson's 4th Division to General Fanshaw's Army, except for the fact that a dispatch or notice had been posted up in the following terms from General Rawlingson, and I quote.

"I cannot allow the 48th Division to leave the 4th Army after seven months of strenuous service, without expressing to all ranks my appreciation and warm thanks for the valuable services they have rendered. After a winter of unexampled severity in indifferent trenches the change to open warfare in March, 1917, found then a high state of efficiency. The skilful leadership and dash display in the capture of Peronne, St Enrolee, Epeny and Guillemont Farms, are deserving of the highest praise and show the standard of efficiency that has been reached, more especially in the close combination of Artillery and the Infantry, is exceedingly high. I congratulate all ranks on the success that they have attained and I shall look forward to some future date when I trust I may have that good fortune to find the Division once more under my Command".

We had not been in our new camp many days before we learned it had got the nickname of Slaughter Wood. It was being regularly shelled by the German batteries, who had got the spot marked for artillery movements as it was adjoining a wooded area for cover. They never let up; it almost became a ritual, like the days of the siege of Poperinghe in 1915, when the positions of our battle lines were much the same. But there was a difference now, because Jerry had developed the technique of night bombing, and he was also using a bomb that burst immediately on impact, with the result that we lost eleven horses in the first raid owing to the immediate explosion, which was cutting them off at the legs.

I took a day off. I had heard that the 17th Division were close too. I was on the go all day, trying to locate anybody whom I might know, but alas to no avail. A number of officers of my pal's unit had gone down to Amiens for the day, and he being an officer's batman, I guess he had gone with them, so after doing Shanks's pony all around Poperinghe I called in a small café and had a meal of fish and chips before making my way back to the wagon lines as it began to get dark. The traffic taking supplies up to the battle front began to roll on the cobbled road up to Ypres. It was two or three miles back to my battery and there was no need to thumb a lift, as the convoy of GS wagons were almost tail to tail, taking supplies to the troops up to the front. I climbed up on the back of a GS wagon (general service wagon) and dropped inside with his load. Oh Boy did I get a surprise! It contained just three shells, which must have weighed at least half a ton each. They were 15 inch shells and they had started out with wooden blocks between them, which had all worked loose and the damn things were rolling about like balls on a billiard table. I sat on one and prized my feet on the outside one to prevent them banging into each other. Was I glad when the GS wagon turned right off the main road into Dicky Bush Road, which was not cobbled, and much softer.

A mile further on we came to a halt near the big Howitzer which was to fire these monsters. About a 100 yards away was another monster, a 9.2 Howitzer, so one could see how they were preparing towards the big day. In fact, if I am not 'jumping the gun', when the big day arrived we were almost axle to axle. As soon as we stopped I slipped under the cover and down the tail board and on my way back to the main road again. (I forgot to mention above that all the GS wagons had canvas covers over the top so you did not see what you were dropping into as you climbed in). I had not far to walk to reach the main Ypres road and got back to my battery all in one piece. I had not been marked absent on my roll call!

We found things had altered from the mobile warfare we had been accustomed to on the Peronne front. We were now being strafed or shelled by day and night, because the Germans had been noticing our activities with men and guns over the past few weeks. We were having a lot more casualties each day, both up at gun positions and also at our wagon lines, with the result that I soon got a permanent position up at the front line, just behind St Julien, where our guns were at that time. As our casualties mounted with the loss of gunners, I soon became No. 2 in the line for the No. 3 seat, which was the gun layer's, and the seat I held throughout the War. It always gave me great pleasure to adjust the line of sight on my No.7, 'Level my Bubble', and pull that lever and say to myself 'Jerry, here I come!'.

We were in action seven days a week now, and also on any night when our infantry sent up an SOS for support. When the Germans put on a night raid, our side did the same, to bring one or two prisoners back for interrogation. The whole front of about 17 miles began to hot up as the big day drew near. Our officers up at the O.P. (observation post) ranged onto our

Canvas-top GS wagons - and New Zealand troops.

Thiepval - advancing under fire.

new targets, marking them out on their maps for the big day. Just across the way, along the Dicky Bush road, another 9.2 Howitzer joined the two big Berthas, a 15 inch and another 9.2. A few days later, a battery of six Howitzers came into action alongside our small 18 pounder. As the big day drew nearer we were practically axle to axle.

The strafing got worse on both sides and casualties also increased among the infantry and the batteries; it was a case again of 'if your name was on it, you'd had it'. It was commonplace to see a small group of troops being blown up in the air. Jerry could not miss hitting some troops and convoys going up to the front line; the roads were choc-a-bloc with troops and material.

Sometimes, when there was a lull in the action, some of the lads would wander across the road to watch the big boys in action. I went across one day. You needed ear plugs to prevent your ear drums from being damaged, but I found it very interesting to be able to watch large shells going through the air. You could follow them right to the end of their trajectory, until they dipped down into the Germans Lines. During the course of the War I was able to notice the trajectory of most calibre guns from 18 pounders up to 15 inch Howitzers. If your eyes were good you could see the shell of a 4.5 Howitzer leave the muzzle of the gun when it was fired, but these were things you had to forget when you were on the receiving end and you had to duck and dive to avoid Jerry's big ones.

There were the 51st Highland Division, the 23rd Division and part of the 7th Division all around us, between St Juliens and the Paschendaele Ridge. They must have lost a lot of troops going up to the support trenches towards the Ridge. Due to the amount of traffic most of the ground had been so churned up that the duck boards and planked roads that the infantry used to walk along to avoid the mud, had disappeared. Now that the rains had set in things were to get even worse, and the conditions became even more hopeless before the Passchendaele Battle was over. The mud and conditions were worse than the Somme - I was in both battles. Whereas the battlefields of the Somme were mostly chalky and allowed the water to run off more quickly, the ground from the Ridge to St Juliens was bogland and held the black mud like gas tar. My division, which was the 48th Division, was frittered away with the corpses of the Belgium, French and Canadian soldiers.

The battle to take this ground had been so fierce they had only had time to bury the dead about a foot below the surface of the ground. At the side of

Mud roads, desolation and a grounded military tractor.

Army mules.

our gun position, which used to be a ploughed field, I saw scores of boots with only the feet in. What had happened to the other parts of the body I will leave you to guess. All the old battlefields were alive with rats. In front of our gun ran a little gully. As the weather worsened the overflow from the small shell holes turned this gully into a little stream, with the result that a number of old corpses became exposed, showing all their bones as white as snow, where the rain water had been flowing through them now for almost three years. One body lay exposed right in front of my gun. The rains had washed the skeleton's bones like ivory. As a matter of fact, his ribs formed a kind of trap which filtered out the brush wood which had flowed down the gully and left a clear space below of clean water into which I used to dip my enamel mug for a drop of water for a shave.

Before many more days passed we were drinking that same shell hole water because the bombardments, which began later, churned up all the ground into a muddy morass and no supply vehicles could get through the mud, not even the water cart. Almost half the brigade went down with dysentery, through having to drink the water out of the shell holes. Almost everything had to be brought up with pack mules - and they were the heroes, if one could apply that description to an animal. We found that a mule could pull or draw almost twice as much as a ordinary horse, but there were times when we had to shoot the poor animals when they really got bogged down in some of the shell holes.

As the end of July 1917 drew near we had two new officers and about 15 gunners and drivers, sent up as reinforcements for the men we had lost around St Julian's. It was really hotting up now and both the German's and our infantry were making raids on each other's trenches to get hold of a prisoner or two for interrogation. It was becoming a nightly operation just before the battle started. On the 30th July 1917 our Section Officer came around to select certain gunners to form a party to go forward that night to prepare a new position for our guns, as the infantry advanced in attack. The following day, 31st July 1917, was to become known as the Battle for the Paschendaele Ridge.

The officer selected to be in charge was one of the reinforcements that had only been with us a few weeks. His name and rank was Lt. A. Burns, and he was a wonderful fellow. He knew his job like an old veteran, although he did not appear to be more than 20 years of age. About, in fact, as old as your humble self who, as usual, seemed always to be picked out for a forward party or a forward gun position - as you will notice throughout my story.

Our party consisted of 24 gunners, with a sergeant named Oakly and Lt. Burns. As we were now a six gun battery it allowed four men for each gun and we were issued with iron rations - the old bully beef and biscuits - a spade and a hundred or so sandbags each, plus the usual respirator, water bottle, and bandoleer, which together made up the approximate load of an infantry man. Not forgetting a rifle between each four men, as being R.F.A. we were not issued with many rifles.

Our journey, which started at midnight from our battery position, was to take us forward about 1½ to 2 miles to the support trenches of the Warwicks, who were on that sector at that time, and we had to wend our way over shell-blasted ground and mud, picking the best track for our guns to come forward and taping it as best we could. You can imagine this was not 'as the crow flies', with Jerry lobbing over 5.9s at that. We were now getting well within rifle range of the Germans, which caused us to do a lot of bobbing and weaving. I could see now the reasons why the Old Soldiers used to say *"Never take a light off a match when lighting a cigarette."* It just gives that sniper time to line you up in his sights and bump you off, because stray ones were flying around very frequently as we neared the German lines. It had taken us the best part of three hours to reach a place where Lt. Burns decided to call a halt.

A few yards away was a massive shell hole, one of many made by Big Bertha. It was partly filled with rain water, but gave us plenty of cover below the surface of the ground, and it allowed all our party to squeeze in, like getting in a bell tent upside down. Our officer said *"Now you can settle down, I have my watch set correctly and will let you know when you can creep to the surface when the fireworks start."* As we were below ground he allowed us to have a smoke and settle down.

The time now was 3.15am. The Sappers and engineers attached to the 48th Division, namely the 474 and 475 companies of R.E.s, had been very helpful in making a track for our guns and transport. They had been out most nights for about a week, under terrific shell fire. They had dumped into the 'cramp holes' anything solid they could lay their hands on, even old discarded rolls of barbed wire, trees, planks and old sandbags, anything to fill up the shell holes to make a passage for the guns to get through. And now we had done as much as we could.

The time was 3.45am, 31st July, and our officer said *"Now lads, you can creep to the surface,"* about twelve inches above us. It was about 3.50am; we had no sooner popped our heads up when we saw two gun flashes

Trenches on the Somme.

Mine craters.

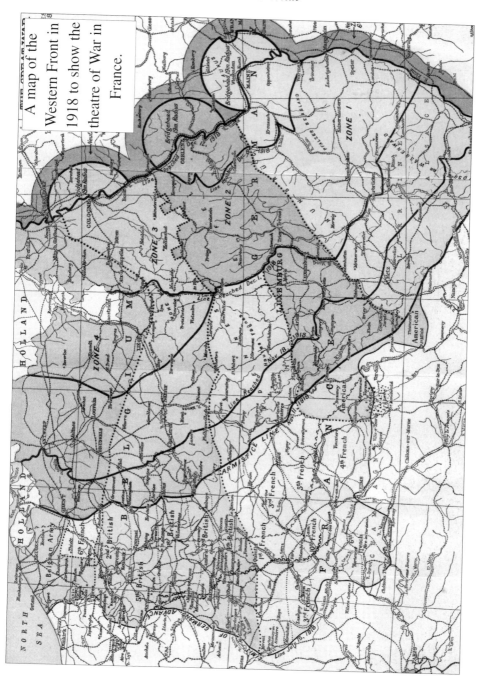

A map of the Western Front in 1918 to show the theatre of War in France.

and in seconds the whole sky was lit up behind us and the thunder of guns was terrific. I had never seen or heard anything like it before in my life.

I had been in the battle of Ypres and the battle of the Somme, but this was greater than either of them. For miles, as far as one could see, the whole front was lit up, and from what I learned later we had attacked the Germans on a front of about 17 miles. I thought the Somme was terrific but then I was only hearing my own battery firing and pulling the lever of my own gun.

Now I had a bird's eye view of most of the battle front, as far as the eye could see, and this was kept up for at least an hour and a half. Our officer had been informed what the procedure was before he left the battery position, and when the barrage was going to be lifted, which was to be (in army terms) a creeping barrage, lifting so many yards per minute, and how any German troops could have lived in that, with all calibre of shells falling within about a yard in between, I do not know. It must have prevented a lot of German gunners from getting into action as our officer gave us the orders to move forward to what had been our original support trenches. The barrage had lifted and our infantry had gone forward to take St Julian and Poelcappelle.

We moved forward in the black mud as it was breaking daylight. The German shelling increased as they retreated towards their second line of defence. We had three men wounded as we pressed forward in the mud, but not seriously, and they were able to trudge along after being bandaged up. As we came towards our old trenches we saw several of our tanks that had been knocked out. A number of them had become really bogged down in the mud, sitting ducks for the German shell fire. We learned afterwards that the land we were moving over, right down the Ridge to St Julians, had been bogland for decades. The Germans chose it for No Man's Land, plus the fact that with them being on the Ridge, they overlooked all our positions of gun emplacements for miles behind our lines.

We were now struggling through the shell holes and the black mud, which stuck to us like glue, until we reached a point near to where our original first line trenches used to be before the attack opened out. Our officers decided that our new gun position was to be at this spot, so each gun place was marked off. It was now hard graft with the gun spades and trenching tools, filling sandbags with our tunics and shirts off, the rain coming down like hell and a thick mist covering the ground like a November morning.

We commenced to build a double row of sandbags to form a gun pit and a certain amount of protection from shell fire, of which we were getting

The total devastation of the War.

plenty at the time. We could see the Sappers and the engineers laying duck boards and plank roads along the shell shattered roads and fields, and these became the only places you could move along, for if you slipped off into the mud you were doomed. Jerry was shelling us with his 5.9s, and as they landed among parties of infantry men and Sappers working on the duck boards, limbs flew into the air like lumps of mud. If anyone had told us before the War that we should have witnessed such slaughter and loss of life and still kept our sanity I would have told them they were talking a load of bullshit. By now, with almost every kind of feeling dried up inside of us, it was as if we had always been used to it.

We were told after the War that the red glow in the sky over Belgium could be seen from the south coast of England, and the heavy bombardments could be heard like thunder in the distance. I never saw so many guns in all my life. We were almost axle to axle at St Julians.

Now we were all moving forward. By about 10.00am, 31st July, the rain had eased off a bit and the mist began to clear. Our guns had arrived and we were lining them up on our targets, as messages began to come through from our O.P. We had built sandbags up to the height of our gun wheels and had covered the gun up with camouflage, which we carried with us. We were ready for action when we heard a plane coming towards us. Suddenly he appeared from nowhere, right on top of us. We could see he was a Jerry by the marking on his wings and as he banked right over us his wing tips were no more the six feet from the ground. Several of us immediately grabbed a rifle and had a pot shot at him, but I am afraid we were unable to hit him.

It would have saved us a lot of trouble if we had been lucky enough to have brought him down, because within half an hour shells began to drop around us, which came closer and closer, and we had no protection other than one or two 'fox holes' we had managed to hurriedly dig in, and they were only about two feet below the surface. Jerry plastered us with his 5.9 Howitzers, both time-bursting and H.E. shells, with the result that we lost four gunners and an NCO within an hour.

One of our men had been hit with a large piece of shrapnel. He was carried towards one of the 'fox holes'. It had scalped him and as we laid him down his brains spewed out over his forehead. I tried to smooth them back again and put the top of his scalp back in place, thinking that he might live! Those are the sort of the things you try to do in our state.

Another of the men who was killed was Mike Chiddy, a bombardier (an NCO with one stripe). He was killed under circumstances which would not happen again in a thousand years. He had been cleaning the gun and oiling the breech and had elevated the nozzle of the gun to enable him to look up through the breech to see if the barrel was clear. At that precise moment a 5.9 time shell had burst about 50 feet up, right in front of the gun he was cleaning, and a piece of shrapnel came straight down the barrel of the gun. He had heard the shell coming and ducked his head down, which happened to be in line with the barrel of the gun. The breech was open at the time, and the piece of shrapnel went right through his head and killed him. I was the first to see him fall, as it was my gun he was cleaning, and my mate Gunner Page and myself laid him out until Jerry had finished strafing us and we buried him just behind our gun. The other gunner, Jack Castello, was already dead when we carried him to the 'fox hole', although we did not know it.

It was action stations as orders kept coming over the line from our O.P. and we commenced to give Jerry a bit back in return. We were in action for most of that day, firing shells as fast as the mules could bring them to us. Between our six guns we must have fired a thousand rounds of ammunition. Even now, only the first day of battle, it was almost impossible for any vehicles to get up to us, owing to the depth of the thick black mud. People talk about the Somme but this was worse. Only mules could struggle through the morass with our supplies. We were in this position for a couple of days, when we had orders to move forward.

The Sappers were all working like Trojans, filling in shell holes, and fixing temporary bridges over the parts of trenches that had been blown to pieces like the one which held the pill boxes. These were the first I had seen, apart from small block houses we encountered on the Somme. There were massive emplacements, in blocks of three, like terraced houses, with a square hole to enter about eighteen inches to two feet square, with room for five or six troops to crawl in, but not enough head room to stand up in. You could either sit up or lie down. They were built in reinforced concrete, which was about 6 feet thick on the top and 4 feet thick on the front facing our side of the line. The entrance, of course, was facing the German rear, and each block had a firing step running along the entire length of the pill box, the top of which came level with the parapet to blend with the line of ground. It also carried steel plates with slots in and even a adjustable table to support a machine gun and give the gunner protection through the slot.

This was what we were moving to for our next position. Yet again we set about protecting our guns with sandbags and camouflage, as Jerry bombarded us with shells of all calibres, including gas shells. The rain tippling down, and the few mule teams which managed to flounder through the mud, only increased it by churning it over and over again. It was Hell. I was going through it at that very moment, and I shall never, never forget it.

Our orders soon began to come through to us over the lines our signallers had lain up to the OP. Our officer had got our guns trained on the German troops, who were on the run, escaping in groups from one point to another. Our bombardment was terrific and helped us to forget the stuff that Jerry was throwing at us. After about two hours of continual gun fire we were given a little respite to sort ourselves out and have a bit of grub, after which we went along to inspect the pill boxes that were just in front of our position, in which we could take cover if the Germans made a counter-attack. This had been the original German front line three days ago. As we got close to them we could see that after years of shelling the largest hole we had made in them was no bigger than what you could put a small barrow into.

We climbed into the trench to investigate the inside of the pill boxes for use as cover. It was a good job we had just satisfied our appetites a short time before, for when we crawled through the opening into the pill boxes I could have heaved my heart out. We had to scrape them off the walls and the stench was terrific. Our infantry, which took the first line of the German trenches, were not taking chances and just threw one, or maybe two, Mills bombs into each block house; and these were the holes we had to sleep in that night.

There were duck boards on the floor of the pill boxes, but the water rose above them owing to the heavy rains. After we had scraped the Germans off the walls, we had to clear the water out before we could get down for a bit of rest. I cannot remember how long it has been since I had my gun boots off, or even any of my clothes; we got down as we got up. We hadn't even got an old candle to run along the seam of our shirt to kill the lice. They were buggers; they would not allow you to doze off even if there was a lull in the shelling.

So the days went on with casualties mounting on both sides, plus the losses from men going down with dysentery because we only had shell hole water for cooking and drinking, because the water carts could not get up through the mud. The poor old mules pulled their hearts out; in some instances, some got so entangled they had to be shot. As we advanced later on, Sappers were busy laying plank roads and filling up shell holes with anything they could lay their hands on. Our position improved as we were getting on higher ground up the Ridge, out of the bogland, and we began to get our water supplies up a bit better.

It was getting towards the end of August. We had already taken St Julian and were making our way towards Poelcappelle, and the 474 and 475 fixed companies of the R.E.s were making it possible for our supplies to get through to the front lines. As records tell, the Sappers, the Gunners and the Drivers had more casualties than the Infantry men in this battle for the Poelcappelle Ridge. We struggled on, hoping this would bring the end of the War and Victory to the allies. The casualties sustained by the 39th Division in the fighting for St Julian were so heavy that the Division was withdrawn during August. Both the 51st Highland Division and the 59th Division had heavy casualties, and we, the 48th Division soon had quite a lot of new faces in our battery.

September came and the rains still kept the ground a sodden morass; our advances were as slow as those in the Somme battle, having to fight for every yard of ground. We were slogging it out through the mud while Jerry was retreating onto drier ground over the Ridge. Our shelling of the Germans increased towards the end of September, and our infantry made a grand assault early in October on the village of Poelcappelle, which they succeeded in taking, bringing our guns well within the range of Poelcappelle. The 11th Division was alongside us and we made an attack on what was known as the Springfield Road and advanced nearly 1,000 yards, just in front of the Langemarck Zonnebeke Road, to the left of Ypres.

This was 1917, and it reminded me that I was in action on the Zillonbeck Road in 1915, which was only a stone's throw from the above. It showed that we had not made much progress on that part of the front over the past two years. However, we were not sorry when we got the orders to move forward from the pill boxes, about a mile towards our objective, which was the Passchendaele Ridge. During the weeks in which we had been using the pill boxes for cover, while the Germans were strafing us, we had other nuisances to contend with besides the lice and rats; namely maggots which, although we had washed the walls down inside the concrete block houses with raw creosote, still crawled all over us.

Then, of course, Jerry, knowing just where the pill boxes were situated, used to shell us with delayed 'armour piercing' shells, which did not explode until they were about 10 feet into the ground, with the result that it was like being in a rowing boat when they dropped one close to us. They used to make a hole like an old fashioned well in the garden. But we were moving on to better ground now, with plenty of old trenches to dig into and make reasonable cover of, along with the sheets of Elephant corrugated iron which they were managing to get up to us at that time. We were still in the same old 'clobber', all torn and muddied up. I could not remember the last time I had my gun boots off, it must have been early in July. In spite of the initial failures, we still had a spirit of optimism, as on the Somme. At Paschendaele, in this confusion of mud and shell fire, we still had that inward feeling of 'God help us' to victory.

After the battle of Passchendaele we had a message of congratulations from the Corps Commander, in which he praised the 11th and 48th Divisions on gaining all their objectives along the whole Corps Front, and another one from the Army Commander, and I quote: '...*captured documents made it clear that this was one of the heaviest blows which the enemy had ever received. A total of over 5,400 prisoners are reported to have been captured.*'

A further report states that the 144th Brigade alone had casualties totalling almost 8,000. All this happened under conditions of heavy rain, with trench boards almost buried under the mud by the continued shelling of the Germans, who played their guns on these tracks our troops were forced to use to get from A to B. Owing to the condition of the ground, it had taken them hours to get into their forward positions in preparation for the attack.

We had now consolidated our position and were knocking on the doors of Paschendaele, which was to be in our possession before many hours had gone around the clock. We could already see the spire of the church of Paschendaele ahead in the distance, rising, not from the mud, but through the trees of the town. Before long it would be in ruins, like the town of Ypres, just on the right, through which I had ridden on the 'limbers' of our guns dozens of times in 1915, coming back from our guns at Zillebeke.

The final battle for the Passchendaele Ridge was about to begin, and as one report puts it, the barrage was of such weight and density as to belittle anything we had seen on the Somme. Certain vital points were neutralised by projectors, which threw up cylinders of gas into the air to land and deliver their contents nearly a mile away. A creeping barrage of heavy shells fell on our objectives a thousand yards away. A standing barrage of shrapnel moved forward in front of us at the rate of thirty yards a minute, and between the two, a searching barrage rolled backwards and forwards to discourage any movement behind their front line posts. It was really hell upon earth, if that is possible, and at the end of the battle for the Ridge, our efforts had cost us over 240,000 casualties, which the records tell included 65,000 dead, a very close second to our losses of the Somme.

The words of a letter by Pte. P. Smith of the 1st Border Regiment, sent to the author of that great story, "The First Day on the Somme", say it all: *"It was pure bloody murder. Douglas Haig should be hung, drawn and quartered for what he did on the Somme. The cream of British manhood was shattered in less than six hours."* I can add two more names to that letter - Rawlinson and Foch. They died in their thousands, those fine men of 1916; they died for the love of their country and a shilling a day.

We were now relieved for a little while from the debacle - about the middle of October 1917 - and sent for a rest to a quieter part of the front - Vimy Ridge!

Pushing through captured land at Vimy Ridge.

Top: A galloping gun team.

Middle: Sappers hard at work in the middle of battle.

Bottom: A glamorised view of an attack at Thiepval.

Chapter 8
Vimy Ridge

We drew out from St Julian and Poelcappelle, joined our wagon lines with the limbers and drivers along the Elverdinghe Road, and made our way along the Ypres Road towards Poperinghe. We turned south on the way to Armentières and passed the old battle fields of Bethune, Loos and La Bassee towards Vimy Ridge, where we were to get the biggest shock our battery was to suffer. During the next 48 hours we were to relieve the Canadian 2nd Division on a front that was supposed to be in quiescence, but our luck was out this time, chiefly through our own fault.

As we got nearer to Vimy our wagon lines were sighted near a place called Fort George, where the Sappers and R.E. were hanging out. We started to settle in to have a feed prepared for us at last, but the following day a party of gunners were picked out to form an advance party to go forward to start to take over the guns from the Canadians, in preparation for a general take over.

The party consisted of one officer, one sergeant, and twenty-four gunners, which included a bombardier from the drivers' section who had been promoted a few weeks before and allowed to join this gun team. His name was Robinson, and this was to be his first time in action. When the next day arrived we were all piled into two GS wagons and we were on our way to a place called the Brick Fields, which ran straight up to the Ridge, a matter of two miles from our wagon lines. On our way up we had to traverse a road that was in full view of the German sausage balloons, but to conceal any movement on the road the R.E.s had fixed a camouflage canvas about ten to twelve feet high, which hid the approach of any vehicles that passed along that road where the area was very flat right up to the Ridge. The roads had the familiar ditches on either side, and on the left hand side of the road, which was on the German side, as we approached Vimy, we passed the grave of Nurse Edith Cavell, with a simple cross on which the following words were roughly printed:

NURSE CAVELL
Was shot here
11th October 1915

I assume her body was removed after the War to a more suitable place.

It was mid afternoon as we approached the gun position under the cover of an old elevated railway siding which ran alongside the Brick Fields towards the German lines, and from the shallow trench enabled us to get to the battery unseen. We found the Canadians a grand lot of lads, who wished us the best of luck as our officer and sergeant made the necessary arrangements to take over. The sergeant busied himself showing the lads around the position and the dugouts the Canadians had built, while our officer went forward with the retiring officer up to the O.P. to see a few shots fired by the battery.

Sergeant Oakley was busy allotting the dugouts to the various subsections. Now these dugouts were on a two tier system. The top portion was supposed to be nine feet below ground, and to us they appeared to be well built and well supported with props and roof supports. As we were the senior subsection, being A subsection, we were given the top storey and B.C.D.E. and F. subsections were given the bottom decks, which branched off from the top storey in two directions.

We all got settled in our new homes in the full confidence of having a nice easy time after the hell up at Passchendaele. All we had to do now was to have our tea ration and wait for the GS wagons to bring up all our kits and blankets. They were not allowed up to the gun position until after dark because Jerry, with his sausage balloons all along the front line, would have made short work of our convoy.

The signal soon went around after dark that the GS wagons had arrived with our rations, kits and blankets, the result being that there was a mad rush to sort out our belongings. Some were using torches, some were using candles and a few were using matches. However, when the melée was all over and everybody seemed to have claimed all their belongings, we started to make up our beds on the floor of the dugouts in preparation for a good night's sleep at last - the first good night's sleep for nearly four months, but I will never forget the next morning as long as I shall live.

We had a quiet night, not even a shell over, and we were ready for our breakfast and a good cup of tea at last. Plenty of rations had been sent up the night before, and it was a full ration for the day ('half a loaf and a dip in the fat'), an event which occurred infrequently for us in 1917, and we could not have enjoyed our breakfast more if the War had been over. But forces were already at work to upset this good feeling.

Bombardier Robinson was a bosom pal of Sergeant Oakley, our number one, and he was instrumental in getting Robinson into the gun team. As we had no orders to go into action as yet, Robinson said to Oakley, *"What about cutting my hair while things are quiet?"* There was an old box on the dugout and the Sergeant said *"Come on Robin, sit on this and I will have a go."*

So he sat on the box and I sat on my haunches close to Robinson's knees, reading an old Western which the Canadians had left behind in a cubby hole cut in the clay. We had lighted a couple of candles. One was stuck on the wall and Gunner Clements was holding the other one. Oakley had been busy with his comb and scissors for about ten minutes and I had been straining my eyes trying to read this book, when Jerry started to lob one or two shells over. They were quite a long way off from our battery and we did not take much notice of them, because we had been used to hearing the cramps of his 5.9 Howitzers continually over the past four months, but as the minutes went by these cramps and explosions began to get bit too close to be comfortable and Robinson said to the Sergeant *"Let's go down below, Oak, it will be much safer down below to finish the job off.",* and the Sergeant said, *"I won't be many jiffys before I've finished it off."*

He had no sooner said it than in it came. I thought the world had come to an end. It came straight through the roof and right through Robinson's body, which was splashed all over the dugout walls and through Sergeant Oakley's legs, who stood on top of the steps, and down to the bottom decks of the dugout. When it exploded and blew the lot in, I was on my feet first and I heard the Sergeant shout down the steps, *"Quick, Austin"* - and I was. I only got down three steps before I found it all blown down below. I shouted to the Sergeant, who was close behind me, *"For Christ sake get back, we're trapped."*

We scrambled back up the steps and could just see a little daylight showing through the hole, the entrance to our dugout. Originally about two feet square, it was now blocked by a chunk of earth which had been blown in it. We rolled it away and the three of us, Sergeant Oakley, Gunner Clements and myself, crawled out and into the trench which ran behind our guns. We were all covered with blood and none of us knew just at the time where we had been wounded. We made our way as best we could to a deep dugout, which was two hundred yards to the rear of our battery and had been built by the Canadians for a Brigade H.Q. It was at least forty feet below ground with compartments for all ranks. Jerry was still strafing us as we made our way to safety, and when we got below, the Canadians, some of whom had not moved out, soon had us all bandaged up and gave us a nice hot drink and allowed us to settle in until dusk, when we were given a lift to the Casualty Clearing Station, better known as the C.C.S., where we were cleaned up and our wounds bandaged. We were then sent down to an advanced dressing station at a safer part of the line.

Not one of the three of us were wounded very seriously. We were what they called walking cases, but there were twenty-one others who would never walk again, because they were all burned alive, all due to our carelessness with flashing lights in our chaotic rush to grab our kit the night before. It was obvious that Jerry had spotted us with his sausage balloons, plus the fact perhaps that our officer had been firing a few rounds to confirm we were on our targets, and that madness had cost us all the lives of five of our gun teams, B,C,D,E and F subsections, plus one out of our subsection A, a gunner called Wilks, who had gone below to the bottom deck to have a natter with a pal.

That catastrophe cost us almost a fifth of our battery's strength, and it all happened in as many seconds. We heard later from some of the Sappers who had tunnelled down to get the bodies out, that the shell that did the damage was an armour piercing delayed action one, similar to the ones they used to strafe us with in the pill boxes at Passchendaele. The Sappers also told us that they had recovered nineteen of the bodies, but ironically the two they never found were Gunner Maynard and Gunner Pugh, two of the quietest men in the battery, who would never say 'Boo' to a goose.

We stayed at the advanced dressing station for a couple of weeks, as our injuries did not warrant them sending us down the line to Blighty. Our wounds were healing up very nicely, and in the meantime we got news that our Division, the 48th Division, along with four more Divisions, among which were the 7th Division and the 23rd Division, were under orders to proceed to Italy to help them out during the Battle of Caporetto and the Asciago Plateau under the Italian General Cadora, who was loosing ground against the Austrians. There were several French Divisions who joined us on this journey to help the Italians out. I think the total of the combined contingent of French and British was about ten divisions. Upon hearing this news, we did not want to be separated from our Division, and on the third week at the dressing station we asked the C.O. if he would discharge us and allow us to join our unit. Although we were bandaged up a bit, he decided to grant our wish and it did not take us long to thumb a lift back to where our battery was stationed, all busy packing for the great Trek.

Everybody was pleased to see us back, alive and kicking, thinking that we had been buried with the other twenty-one gunners. We were able to give them a true account of the debacle which had befallen us at Vimy Ridge. A horror which happened in sixty seconds - to loose twenty-one of your pals

No. 115
5 1405
(If replying, please quote
above No.)

Army Form B.104—81.

R. H. & R.F.A. Record Office,

Woolwich

Nov 9, 1917.

SIR, ~~OR MADAM,~~

I regret to have to inform you that a report has been received from the War Office to the effect that (No.) 107274 (Rank) Gunner

(Name) Heraty A. J.

(Regiment) R.F.A. was wounded

on the 19th day of Oct 1917.

It has not yet been reported into what hospital he has been admitted, nor are other particulars yet known, but directly any further information is received it will be at once communicated to you.

I am to express to you the sympathy and regret of the Army Council.

Yours faithfully,

LEAVE OR DUTY RATION BOOK
SOLDIER OR SAILOR.

IF FOUND, RETURN TO ANY FOOD OFFICE.

Serial No. S 8 No. 012733

1. Holder's Name Heraty A J   Rank 107274
2. Unit or Ship 911 Bde R.F.A.   Number Gunner
3. Proceeding from ITALY
4. Beginning of leave or duty
5. End of leave or duty
6. Is holder proceeding at end of leave or duty on Active Service Abroad or Service Afloat? No
7. Signature and Rank of Officer issuing   CAPTAIN, R.F.A.
8. Unit or Ship of Officer issuing ADJUTANT 241 (S.M.) BRIGADE R.F.A.

N. 9.

forever - will live in my mind until I die.

We were soon settled in again, and of course I was to be the senior gunner of our team. I got my old job back as limber gunner, which meant I was responsible for the gun and gun limber to be kept clean and well oiled, and which stood me in 'good stead', as the saying goes, at a later date.

Chapter 9
Our Journey to the Italian Front

We started to prepare for our long journey to Italy, which included the securing of mule teams and guns. All of us were issued with two of everything of underclothing, and these included the army issue of the long, all woollen pants - long johns, as they were termed. The under-vests were also all wool. The troops hated them, especially the long johns, with the result that they were glad to hand them over to me for cleaning rags for the guns. Not having any kit bags to stuff them in, I found the cages under the gun limbers very handy, and I packed all the cages full of underwear - a place where nobody looked only the limber gunner. I had ideas which I never told anybody about; they were to hold me in 'good stead' as I said at the end of the last chapter; I had visions of augmenting my Army pay of sixpence a day.

It was now the middle of November 1917, and things were looking a little brighter for us. Our rations had reverted to the old full ration of 'half a loaf and a dip in the fat', and our wagon lines had been pulled back to a small town called St Pol, in preparation for the treck to Amiens. Here we were to entrain for Italy.

It was like being in another world for the time being, out of range of Jerry's 5.9s, having a full belly, and being able to call into an estaminet for a glass of French beer. We were beginning to loose that feeling of insanity and to get back to normal, with that feeling of 'it's a treat to be alive'.We were getting all the rules and regulations dished out to us again and were put back on the old spit and polish routine.

Everything had to be in tip top form for our entry into this new theatre of war and we all worked very hard on polishing and burnishing the harness and guns. Our turnout was a credit to our C.O. when we left St Pol to entrain on our journey to Italy in horse boxes. We were to stay in them for over a week, to eat sleep and make merry, if you follow what I mean, and as I have mentioned in my earlier chapters the French railways had only two speeds, slow and stop. Some of the stops made up for the lack of corridor carriages. We made our way south, passing the headquarters of the French Army at Chentilly Chateau, near the outskirts of Paris and down to Marseille and along the French Riviera, keeping close to the Mediterranean all the time.

The sea was just as blue as they paint it in pictures, and we came to a stop right opposite the Bank of Monte Carlo, which we could see quite

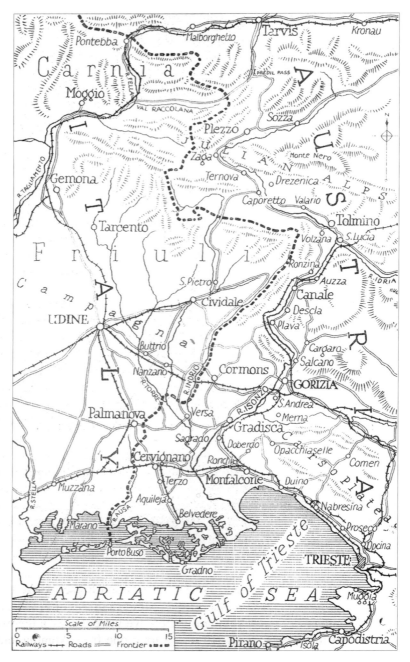

The Italian Isonzo Front.

clearly about half a mile from the train. We thought it wonderful to be so near to a place that had such a reputation. We were still being drawn by the old steam engines and being shunted on to sidings from time to time to allow faster traffic a clear line, and at these it allowed the cooks to make us a cup of char, made with clean water instead of having to run up to the front of the train and turn on the hot water tap on the engine's boiler - quite easily done even if the train was on the move. But as we got nearer the Italian Frontier we were switched to electric railways, and I remember quite well going through the longest tunnel I had ever known. It must have been fifteen miles long. Going through the Alps, we were in this tunnel for about twenty minutes at a good speed, and as we emerged from it, the seasons seemed to have turned around.

It was winter when we left Vimy Ridge and a few days later we seemed to be running into summer again as the train sped on all around the Gulf of Genoa, still running alongside the Mediterranean, right up to Genoa, through the Italian Riviera, which was a lovely sight for us to see after what we had been through, even if we were still in horse boxes.

We turned North after passing through Genoa and made our way to Milan, passing Lake Garde and Verona then across towards Vicenza, a city I was to visit later on. All the way up from Genoa they gave us V.I.P. receptions at every stop, and if it happened to be in a station they were lowering baskets of fruit and foods of all descriptions on pieces of rope from the bridges above, even bottles of vino galore. Incidentally, wine was very cheap in Italy at that period of time. It was only two and a half cents (about two and a half pence in our money) for one litre. In other words, you could go to a café and get bleary-eyed for two and a half pence.

In the meantime, between stations and stops, the long johns, still stuffed in the cages, began to stand me in 'good stead'. At each stopping place, which occurred very frequently between the stations, I was selling pants and vests like hot cakes, for 5 lira each. By the time we reached the centre of Italy and Calogna Venata, about 50 kilometres north east of Mantua, where we were to detrain, I was pretty flush, which allowed me to stand drinks all round for the lads, although I never let on where the money had come from, and they never asked, so everything was OK!

From now on we were busy unloading guns and horses ready for our trek towards our new billets at a place called Monteccio Majoria, which was a few miles south of Grappa Mountains, where we were to stay a few weeks before we went into action. The trek was a long one from Mantua and the

Italian people seemed very relieved and delighted to see us on the road with our smart turnout of guns and horses, all gleaming in the sunshine. The Italians made such a fuss of us, we might have won the War! We must have travelled for nearly two days on the road and we could always see the Grappa Mountains in the distance, which never seemed to come any nearer. We eventually reached the foothills and our new wagon lines at the lovely village of Monteccio. We were all beginning to think that being in the army was not too bad after all. We had plenty of rations now that our supplies were catching up with us, and we had a village bakehouse only few yards away. The weather was simply glorious and everything in the garden was lovely, as they say. Our food was not too bad, only the meat was so tough you could neither get your teeth into it, nor digest it. The lads used to nail it to the barn doors for the C.O. to see for himself; but nevertheless the barns we were sleeping in were clean and we were able to put up two tier beds with a bit of timber and wire-netting.

We were in this little place for about three weeks, trying to socialise a bit with the Italian people, and trying to say 'Bon Journo' and 'Bon A Sarah' as it sounded to us, and learning to say 'Uno' 'Due' and 'Tre', etc., until the time came for action stations. The Italian lorries were Fiats, specially built with five or six forward gears for mountain climbing They were to take us right to the top of the Grappa Mountains, 7000 or 8000 feet above sea level, and it took the best part of a day to arrive at the place where we could look across the valley into Austria.

We had left the plain, where it was scorching hot and climbed up to the top of the mountain, where the snow was above knee deep. Here you picked your way, for if you slipped off the beaten track you would be swallowed up. On the way up the hairpin bends were breathtaking and sometimes they could not get around on one lock and had to reverse. When we got near the edge you could look down about 2000 to 3000 feet below. One little mistake on the driver's part and you had had your 'chips'. The Italians reckoned they averaged one lorry a day lost over the top through the War!

The Italian gunners welcomed us with open arms, and could not do enough for us. They had plenty of rations and gallons - or litres - of vino. They had built dugouts with layers of pine tree logs that could withstand direct hits from small calibre shells. The Italian soldiers stayed with us for about three days, because it was all hands to the wheels to change over the guns, and at night time they entertained us with songs about General Cadorna (who was to fall in disgrace over the Caporetto Battle), and drinking vino.

The next day was a clear and sunny one. As we looked across at the enemy-held territories, the views were glorious, with snow-capped mountains towering in the background. Below lay a small village, with its white buildings standing out against the green fields. From what we could see, we came to the conclusion that it was a position of stalemate between the Austrians and the Italians, with not a shot being fired by either side. There could hardly be a greater change from the desolation of the tree-scorched and muddy terrain of the Ypres Salient over which we had floundered a few months before.

This was where I saw my first glimpse of a polecat. They were very horrid looking creatures. Whether it was they that were eating rats, or vice versa, I do not know, but there were plenty of them about. I had been allocated the top bunk in the dugout, and the buggers used to keep me awake in the night, running backward and forwards over a spar of wood which ran above my head.

This new war began to change when the officers went up to the O.P. and started to range on different targets, and we soon livened the Austrians up a bit and let them see that we wanted to finish the whole thing. Our other divisions, five British and five French, did the same and the Austrians found they had to call on Germany for a few divisions to stem the tide. Taking the offensive by either side seemed out of the question, because of the terrain, and the fact that we were in clouds for days at a time. Both sides seemed to be satisfied to hold their own for the time being and the Austrians concentrated on the lower Plateau down at Asiago on the Piave, and Montello, which they did with a view to cutting us off in the foot hills of the Grappa Mountain.

After about six weeks on the top of the Grappa we were withdrawn and sent South East down on the Asiago Plateau. We settled in a little village near the town of Treviso, which was only about twenty miles from Venice, but that was the nearest we ever got to it. We were there for a few weeks to prepare for the battle of Asiago.

It was May 1918, and the weather was glorious. The maize was ripening in fields which were divided by rows of walnut trees, up which grapevines were trained to grow. We used to lay under the trees eating the black grapes until our tummies ached. The bunches were nearly two feet long. It made one wonder how such a weight of fruit could hang on one stem. In the evening we used to join the family of the farm and go into the cow shed trying to pick up the lingo and be understood.

Troops in the mountains.

Motor supply columns in the Italian campaign.

The Italians were very backward as regards to agriculture. Their ploughs were not very modern and were drawn by oxen, and the farm hands, when they had not much to do in the farmyard, used to kick off their sandals, which had no heels, and with no stockings on, used to jump in the big vat which stood under a large shed and tread the grapes with their feet to squeeze out the juice. They were even using horses on the tread mill to operate the grinding machinery, and I never saw any coal all the time I was in Italy. All their cooking was fuelled by wood burning.

With such nice weather and being out of range of the Austrian guns and shelling, the following three weeks seemed to slip by quicker than a shell, and we were on our way back across the Asiago Plateau and through the Trentino Valley and up into the mountains again, but not so high. We left our wagon line in the foot hills of the Trentino and made our way up into the mountains to between 3000 and 4000 feet above sea level. This entailed a steady climb for two to three hours in our Fiat wagons. The guns and limbers were to follow, drawn by special lorries for mountain climbing and the drivers were to follow on with the pack mules and the stores from the wagon lines so that they were within about two miles of our gun positions.

It was slow work getting everything into the correct place for the drivers and mules to be protected from the Austrian shell fire. It entailed climbing and struggling up a mule track for about fifteen miles, to a part of the plateau where it was safe. The gunners and their equipment had to go right to the top of the Asiago Plateau, facing the Austrians on another range about four or five miles as the crow flies. Little smallholdings and farm houses dotted down the mountain sides, with small villages nestling in the bottom of the valley. Each side had concealed guns and search-lights on the mountain sides and believe me, you will never guess the next move. The powers that be had decided that one gun was to be sent forward down the mountain to a position just behind our support trenches, and overlooking the little village of Caesura.

Was it our gun? Well if you tried another guess you would be wrong, for it was Sergeant Oakley and our gun team that had been chosen to go forward. It seemed that our C.O. had got it into his head that we possessed charmed lives. But as I have said before in this story, if your name is on it, you've had it. Our gun was ranged on the Caesura Switch and the Lemerle Switch, a point that had got a reasonable track road suitable for small calibre guns to be manoeuvred into position.

This part of the Plateau was very broken ground, composed of rough stone outcrops with several small hillocks rising to about 100 feet. We had plenty of log dugouts in which to take cover. The mountain sides were thick with pine trees of all sizes, so we were not short of timber to conceal our dugouts up to any depth. We had been in this position for about two weeks and our officer up at the O.P. had been doing a bit of shooting on various targets each day. I well remember our C.O. coming up to visit our position with our regular battery officer and bringing General Strong along for a bit of sniping with an 18 pounder. Our C.O. at that time was Colonel Sankey, a member of the giant sugar combine, and he had been sending orders down the wire to our gun to fire on various targets, to let General Strong see how accurate we were with our shooting. Suddenly the order came down to a fresh target which swung our gun to the extreme right and the order came through after the first shot - *"Three rounds gun fire"* - and three it was, *"Pronto"*. A few moments later the telephone buzzer went again. It was Colonel Sankey asking Sergeant Oakley who the 'gun layer' was, and when he told him that it was yours truly he said, *"Put Gunner Heraty on the line"*.

I said *"Hello, Sir, Gunner Heraty speaking"*, he said *"I want, on behalf of General Strong, to congratulate you on the speed and accuracy which accounted for 50% of your target"*. (Inwardly I felt that may mean a stripe for me but it didn't). We heard later, from our battery officer, that he had been taking a pot at about half a dozen Austrians - infantry men who were making their way to their support trenches, and as we learned later there must have been hundreds of these troops passing down the track for days on end, because the following week the Austrians made a terrific assault on our Sector which came to be known as the Battle of the Asiago Plateau.

It was June 1918, and the 5th Division and the 41st Division were sent back to France, following the big offensive by the German armies in France in the spring, which left only the 7th Division, the 23rd Division and the 48th Division. In addition we had a flu epidemic on our hands, which had depleted our strength by at least 25%, when the Austrians struck.

It was about 3.00am when they started to bombard us with all calibre of guns. Amongst them were the small mountain guns with which they were strafing us with gas shells. They had found a weak spot on the right of our position quite close to the Cesuna Switch, which the Warwicks were holding next to the 7th Division. Believe me, it was almost as bad as Passchendaele in its ferocity and they kept it up for almost four hours. The Austrians had been searching us out with their searchlights for two or three nights prior to that bit of shooting we had done when our C.O. was sniping at them. It was

Italian artillery on mountain road.

Guns at the Italian front.

so powerful that you could pick three-penny bits off the ground. We had to keep quite still, like broken trees, when they were using the lights. Our gun was well camouflaged with netting and green shrubbery but I think he had spotted us doing a bit of night firing, which we had to carry out more as a nuisance mission to let him know we had got the Casuna Switch track covered.

When he had opened out his terrific bombardment he let us know he had got us spotted. We could not move out of our dugout. It was devastating. Shortly after he had eased off a bit we began to see our infantry retreating up the mountainside, shooting their way out as they worked up through the barbed wire entanglements. This told us that the Austrians had broken through and were only about 200 yards away, so between us we rushed to the gun and took the remaining pin out of the breech block and removed the block. We also took the No 7 dial sight off the sliding carriage and away we scampered, up the mountain. The higher we climbed, the more we came under the Austrian rifle sights and his machine guns, only two hundred yards away. Our only shelter was offered by young pines, only about eighteen inches high.

God must have been on our side that day. We kept dodging about up the hillside until we reached the top and over we went. We were now safe and out of reach. Sergeant Oakley was carrying the dial sight and Gunner Page was carrying the breech block. We made our way back to the gun position and reported to our officer, who went into the C.O.s dugout to report what had happened. The officer came back and told us we were to go and see the C.O., who was Lt. Col. Sankey. We could see by his face that he was not in a very good mood at hearing what had happened, and he said to the Sergeant *"What have you done to your gun, Oakley?"*. The Sergeant told him we stuck it out as long as we could. Since we had only one gun between us to hold back the Austrians, we had to retreat or be taken prisoners.

The C.O. was in a real rage. He said to the Sergeant *"Now Sergeant Oakley you go back straight away and take your men with you. Go and get your gun back."*

We had to obey orders. We went back and as it turned out, our luck had changed. The Warwicks and the Gloucesters had made a counter attack in the same afternoon. With the support of the 7th Division they had pushed the Austrians right back again beyond their original first line trenches, capturing the village of Cesuna and the mountain tracks they had been using to supplying their troops in the trenches.

We carried on, back to the top of the plateau and down the mountain side to where we had left our gun. We had plenty of support now. Fresh reinforcements filed up the mountain road with machine guns and automatic rifles, and when we got to our dugout, there was one dead Austrian soldier inside. He appeared to have been on the scrounge for food when he was knocked off. Outside were about a dozen of the enemy who had been mown down by the Warwicks as they counter-attacked. We found our gun quite serviceable. Although they had made an attempt to set it on fire, it was not long before we had fixed it up again and were ready for action.

I have often thought about that day in two lines of poem my Dad used to quote. It goes as follows: "He that fights and runs away, Lives to fight another day." I do not know who wrote it but it worked for us.

The following day we had orders to go forward with our counter-offensive to follow up our initial strike across the Ghelpac Ravine and enter the Austrian's second line of trenches near Canove, where I was wounded for the third time by a piece of shrapnel which hit me in my left leg, right in the fleshy part of my thigh. This put me in the 'almost rans' for the time being and prevented me being 'in at the death' because we had got the Austrians on the run for the last time in the Great War.

They sent me down to an advance dressing station at Montabelluna, about seven kilometres from Treviso, on the Piave Plain. Here I was to stay in tents for the next four or five weeks. The influenza epidemic was still very bad, for out of a quota of two hundred patients they were losing an average of twenty-four a day with flu deaths. I was in bed next to two Indian civilians. How they got mixed up with the Austrian prisoners we had taken at Casuna, I don't know, but they both died of flu at the side of me. I heard from some of the wounded Warwicks that were sent down here, that our division, the 48th Division, had lost about 70 officers and almost 1000 other ranks, but the Austrians had lost more than us. In fact, we took almost that number in prisoners alone, plus mountain guns and "Flammenwerfers", not to mention machine guns and other equipment.

As the wounded continued to arrive they told us how the Warwicks and the Gloucesters of the 48th Division were chasing the Austrians up through the mountain passes towards the Austrian border, and how the Chief of Staff, General Commander General Cavan, had issued orders to all ranks to keep the enemy on the run, using the officers' slogan of 'Press on Regardless'. This left me longing to be amongst them, so as to be in at the kill. Since my wound had not been a serious one, they let me loose after about five weeks.

Form E.

WAR OFFICE,

FINSBURY COURT,

FINSBURY PAVEMENT,

LONDON, E.C.2,

Any further letter on this subject should
be addressed to—
The Secretary,
War Office,
Finsbury Court,
Finsbury Pavement,
London, E.C.2,
and the number below quoted.

9th December 1918

C. 2. Casualties E.

No. 751221

Reg. No. 107274 Rank Gnr Name A. J. Heraty

Regiment Royal Field Artillery

Sir,

In reply to your enquiry of the 20th November 1918 I am directed to inform you that the above-named soldier has been officially reported as having been injured on the 1st October 1918 and rejoined his unit on the 13th October 1918

This is the latest information regarding this soldier which has been received.

Future enquiries of this kind should be addressed to :—

The Officer in Charge of Records,

Royal Field Artillery Record Office,

Woolwich Dockyard Woolwich SE.

who is in possession of the latest information obtainable respecting soldiers of this regiment.

I am, Sir,

Your obedient Servant,

B Grindle

Mr a Heraty
15 Bailey St
Newcastle Staffs

(8 47 35) W1255—HP2573 50,060 5/18 HWV, (P705) H18/196

116

But my problems were just beginning; finding your battery in that mix up on the Asiago Plateau was not going to be easy.

Anyhow I was on my way again, thumbing a lift when I could, and that night I approached the sergeant of an R.E. Company, on the way up to the Asiago Plateau as reinforcements for road-making. I told him I was on my way to join my battery and asked him to allow me to stay the night with his lot. Things were moving fast now and after having a bit of breakfast the next morning with the R.E.s, I was on my way again, jumping on all kinds of transport for a lift, whether French or Italian, until I reached our wagon lines in the foot hills of the Asiago Plateau. Here I got lots of news about my battery. I learned from the drivers who returned with the pack mules that our division was leading the attack and that we were well in front of the French divisions and the Italian division. I was told that our division had to mark time until the other divisions caught up, which gave me a chance to catch up with them as they were making their way through the Granezze Valley. This led through the mountains to Asiago proper. When we caught up with them the drivers gave us all the news and said that the narrow roads were treacherous to negotiate, but things seemed to be going well for us and batches of Austrian prisoners were continually finding their way down the mountain tracks.

It was now August 1918, and the Austrians seemed to make every effort to hold on to what they had taken of the Italian Frontier. Our Divisions had found it hard going in the mountainous country. They were not trained like the Alpine troops and it was much more difficult than trench warfare in a flat country. With various ingenious methods and the will to conquer all obstacles, we let the Austrians see we meant business.

Things went quiet for a week or two, until around the middle of September 1918, when the enemy made a concerted attack on our sector and broke through our lines, capturing our front line trench near Cesuna and penetrating up to about a 1000 yards into our lines. The battle lasted all that day and throughout the night. When it quietened off a bit at about 7.30am, our Commanding Officer called upon one or two brigades of the 7th Division, who were lying in support about two miles back. Along with the 23rd Division and the 48th Division they had made a counter attack and pushed the Austrians right back again, taking about 200 prisoners and releasing a number of our men who had been taken prisoners the day before.

The attack was a complete success. According to information that officers obtained from the prisoners, it seemed as though the Austrians were in a desperate plight. Their food was getting very scarce and some of the infantry men had to resort to cutting the hind quarters off their horses for food. Combined with other information prisoners had disclosed, our officers put two and two together and the 'Head-Brass', or Chief Commander, who at that time was Earl Cavan, decided that we must prepare to assemble our forces for a concerted attack against the Austrians. The same methods were used as the Austrians had tried at Caporetto in the latter part of 1917, when they crossed the Brenta and Piave rivers to cut off the Italian armies on Asiago Plateau. This tactic had nearly lost the Italians' war.

I said earlier that the French sent five divisions to Italy, which was wrong, as they sent seven divisions along with five divisions by the British, but two divisions were sent back with General Plummer. The 5th and 41st were to help on the Western Front after the great German attack in 1918. That left us with about ten divisions made up of British and French and about nine or ten divisions of Italian troops to make the final assault on the Austrians.

Although we did not know at this time, the Austrians had made their last fling on the Asiago Plateau, when they tried to break through to the Trentino Valley. The powers that be were working out a strategy to make a prolonged and massive attack against the Austrians, which turned out to be highly successful. When it was all over, it seemed (this was my own opinion) that it was the Battle of Caporetto in reverse.

We built up a striking force over the weeks that followed, holding the Austrians at bay, and still keeping up our raiding parties, bringing prisoners back for interrogation and making attacks on what we thought were weaknesses in their defence. These continued throughout the summer. We were approaching October 1918 and still nobody seemed to know when we were going to attempt this breakthrough. Although we did not know it at the time, this was to be our last battle of the Great War, the Battle of Asiago.

October came and it was nearing the end of the month when things began to hot up. On Saturday 26th October 1918, our barrage opened on the enemy and attacked their bridgeheads across the Brenta and Piave rivers. The 7th Division and the 23rd Division captured both of them and gained a bridgehead across the Piave River near Montella. The two British divisions formed part of an Italian British Corps which came under General Cavan and General Dios, the Italian General who had taken over from General Cadorna in 1917. When our troops had consolidated their bridgehead they made their way to the lower peaks of the Asiago, captured Mt Catz and skirted around the deep ravine of Val d'Assa. Making their way over the narrow passes, they fought to capture Caldonazzo, which the Austrians were using as their main supply route through to the Brenta and Trentino Valleys. We had got them on the run and there was no stopping our troops now. The Austrians were becoming demoralised and leaving loads of their equipment behind such as machine guns, mortars, ammunition and stores. The prisoners were finding their way down the mountain passes, some parties consisting of 100 to 200 men with guards. Gangs of a dozen or so found their own way down unattended, glad to know it was all over as far as they were concerned.

Our next objective was the town of Campovorere up the Val d'Asso and on to Caldonazzo, which was on the Austrian border. After passing through Val Portule road junction on the Val d'Asso road, about five miles from Asiago, the place looked like Ypres after our continual shelling at Caldonazzo, and we found vast amounts of army stores in the sheds adjacent to the railway. There were over 200 sheds prepared for blowing up, containing several thousands of machine guns and rifles and army equipment of all kinds. In a huge yard near the railway were several hundred wagons, most of them packed with harnesses, all left intact.

It was now the 4th November 1918, and the Chief Officers, including Lord Cavan, were signing the important cessation papers for unconditional surrender, and our war with the Austrians was over. The 48th Division was the first division to enter enemy territory and it was the Chief Officers of the 48th Division who signed the Surrender of Austria. That same day General Walker, who was the Division Commander, issued this order of the day -

"Officers, NCO's and men of the 48th Division, your achievements during the past few days of the most profound military events deserve unstinted praise. After fourteen weeks of warfare and arduous work, chiefly at night, combined with frequent raids of the most difficult, though successful nature, you have undertaken an attack on a front originally allocated to two Divisions, against what ought to have been impregnable mountain positions, you have swept away the enemy rear guards and acting as the vanguard of the 6th Italian Army. You have advanced so rapidly and with such resolution that the retiring enemy have had no time to reform and have left over 20,000 prisoners, hundreds of guns and immeasurable booty in the hands of the Division. The mere performance of the march in the time and under the conditions you endured would have been, even without opposition, considered a creditable feat. You can justly claim that the favourable situation of the Italian Armies on this front at 15:00 hours

today, when one of the most memorable armistices in History was signed, is largely due to your exertions and resolution. As your Division Commander I cordially thank you. 4th November, 1918, H.B. Walker, Major General Commanding the 48th Division".

So we had signed the armistice seven days before Germany gave up France. As our journey was at an end as far as the Austrians were concerned, and the occupying forces were left in charge, our job now was to get back through the mountains and on to the plains again, in search of a suitable place for our division to lick our wounds and recuperate. After miles of travelling we landed in a place called Tezze, a lovely little village which was to be our home until we were demobbed - but not before a little 'spit and polish'.

On the 27th November 1918, we had to polish and burnish everything, ready for a special inspection by the King of Italy. After that was over it was all plain sailing and we were back to square one with the usual parades, which meant reveille and the horses fed and watered before anybody else in the morning. Ater grooming the horses we were free for most of the day, and as Christmas was drawing near we had visions of turkey and plum pudding.

Life seemed to take on a new look now, as we were able to go out at night and have plenty of vino if we were flush, it was only $2^{1/2}$ pence a litre. Best of all, we were able to wash our shirts a bit more often now. There were plenty of streams running through the village and these gave us a better chance of keeping ourselves a little cleaner and more comfortable.

Christmas came and went, and things continued to improve as our mail was beginning to catch up with us. Everybody was looking forward to the day when his name would be called out on the list to be sent back home. It appears that seniority was the order of the day, and that 'Key Men' in industry were to be released first. I knew that I fell into that category so maybe I would not have to wait long. However, waiting still seemed such a long while, but eventually my day came along, in February 1919. I joined a party for the rail-head to proceed to England. I said goodbye to all the pals I had made in the battery and I was on my way back home.

They took us to the rail head at a place called Theine, where we boarded a train through Italy and then across France to the port of Le Havre. From here we crossed to Southampton and then trained to Waterloo. There we were put on a train which was to take us up into Yorkshire, to a place called Clipstone. This was the depot from which we were to be de-mobbed. They gave us new underclothes and a suit from the 30/- tailors, plus a trilby and a pair of boots, plus a month's pay, a month's ration money, and that was your lot - for what?

To conclude my little story; I hope my readers will appreciate that I have no access to Divisional or Brigade secrets or reports, but what I have written here, apart from a couple of quotes, I have seen and gone through. And what have I got? Well, I'll tell you.

I have got my attestation papers from the day I enlisted, and also my discharge certificate and all that goes between them. Namely, I have all the buff forms from the War Office which informed them each time I was wounded, which was on three occasions. I also have the buff Forms from the Records Office awarding me my medals, I have my Ration Book for the First World War, also my Unemployment Book and also an item which I do not think any other soldiers retained - the labels (luggage) which were tied on to your buttons when you were a casualty on the battlefield.

I have my Pal. As I was in two strange divisions, he was the only man that I met throughout the War whom I already knew - at Armentières. He calls to see me about once a month. He is 83 years of age and goes old time dancing three nights a week. He is fit as a fiddle and his name is Harry Woodcock. He lives at Lightwood Road near Longton.

When I feel 'down in the dumps' at times, I usually hum that old war song to myself:

"Pack up your troubles in your old kit bag,
and smile, smile, smile."

and sometimes I repeat a line from an old song, or poem, I don't know which:

"Old soldiers never die they only fade away."

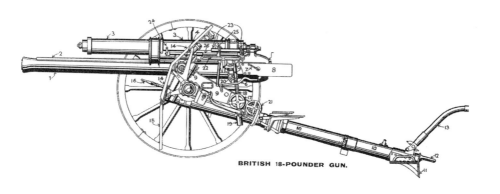

BRITISH 18-POUNDER GUN.

Z 48681

H. & R.F.A. Records.

CERTIFICATE of* { ~~Discharge~~ / Transfer to Reserve / ~~Disembodiment~~ / ~~Demobilization~~ } on Demobilization.

Army Form Z. 21.

Regtl. No. 107274 Rank. Gunner

Names in full. Heraty Austin James
(Surname first)

Unit and Regiment or Corps
from which
~~*Discharged~~
Transferred to Reserve } **R.H. & R.F.A.**

Enlisted on the 6th September 1915

For R H & R F Artillery
(Here state Regiment or Corps to which first appointed)

Also served in ....

Only Regiments or Corps in which the Soldier served since August 4th, 1914, are to be stated.
If inapplicable, this space is to be ruled through in ink and initialled.

†Medals and
Decorations
awarded during
present engage-
ment
Medals for present campaign not yet awarded.

*Has
~~Has not~~ } served Overseas on Active Service.

Place of Rejoining in }
case of emergency } Catterick Medical Category. A.1.

Specialist Military }
qualifications } Nil Year of birth. 1896.

He is* { ~~Discharged~~ / Transferred to Army Reserve / ~~Disembodied~~ / Demobilized } on 25th February 191 9.
~~Beverley~~
in consequence of **Demobilization.**

For **Colonel.** Signature and Rank.

Officer i/c **R.H. & R.F.A.** Records. **Woolwich.** (Place).

* Strike out whichever is inapplicable. † The word "Nil" to be inserted when necessary.

(20996). Wt. W 8211—P.P. 2329. 3,000m. 1/19 D & S. (E 1256.)

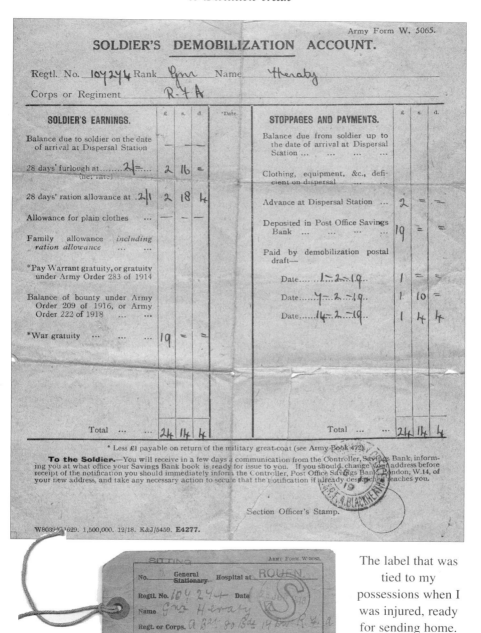

Army Form W. 5065.

SOLDIER'S DEMOBILIZATION ACCOUNT.

Regtl. No. **104244** Rank **Gnr** Name **Heraty**

Corps or Regiment **R.F.A.**

SOLDIER'S EARNINGS.	£	s.	d.	*Date.	STOPPAGES AND PAYMENTS.	£	s.	d.
Balance due to soldier on the date of arrival at Dispersal Station					Balance due from soldier up to the date of arrival at Dispersal Station			
28 days' furlough at........2/=...... (net rate)	2	16	=		Clothing, equipment, &c., deficient on dispersal			
28 days' ration allowance at .2/1	2	18	4		Advance at Dispersal Station ...	2	=	=
Allowance for plain clothes ...	—	—	—		Deposited in Post Office Savings Bank	19	=	=
Family allowance *including* *ration allowance*					Paid by demobilization postal draft—			
*Pay Warrant gratuity, or gratuity under Army Order 283 of 1914					Date.... ..1.-.2.-.19..	1	=	=
Balance of bounty under Army Order 209 of 1916, or Army Order 222 of 1918					Date.....4.-.2.-.19..	1	10	=
					Date.....14.-.2.-.19..	1	4	4
*War gratuity	19	=	=					
Total	24	14	4		**Total**	24	14	4

* Less £1 payable on return of the military great-coat (see Army Book 472).

To the Soldier.—You will receive in a few days a communication from the Controller, Savings Bank, informing you at what office your Savings Bank book is ready for issue to you. If you should change your address before receipt of the notification you should immediately inform the Controller, Post Office Savings Bank, London, W.14, of your new address, and take any necessary action to secure that the notification if already despatched reaches you.

Section Officer's Stamp.

W8039 1629. 1,500,000. 12/18. K&J/5459. E4277.

SITTING

Army Form W 3083.

No.	General Stationary	Hospital at ROUEN
Regtl. No. 104244		Date
Name Gnr Heraty		
Regt. or Corps. A 321 80 Bty 14 Bde R.F.A		
Name of Ship ST ANDREW		

The label that was tied to my possessions when I was injured, ready for sending home.

Statement Showing Articles of Clothing and Necessaries—continued.

	Mounted Services.	Dism'd Service (except Killed Regts.)	Killed Regts.	REMARKS.
COMB, HAIR. ...	1			
DISCS, IDENTITY, No. 1 } GREEN, with cords. } DISCS, IDENTITY, No. 2 } RED.	1			
FORK. ...	.			
GARTERS, pair ...	.			
HOLDALL ...	1			
HOUSEWIFE ...	1			
HOSETOPS, pair ...	1			
KNIFE, TABLE ...	.			
LACES, 30 in., pair ...	1			
LACES, 50 in., pair ...	1			
RAZOR AND CASE ...	1			
SHIRTS, FLANNEL ...	1			
SOCKS, WORSTED, pairs ...	1			
SOAP, cake ...	1			
SPOON. ...	1			
SPURS, JACK, pairs ...	.			
TOWEL, HAND ...	1			
VEST, WOOLLEN ...	1			} Not in Summer.
WOOLLEN GLOVES OR } MITS., pair.	1			
DRESSING, FIELD ...	1			
PAY BOOK ...	1			
HAVERSACK. ...	1			
TINS, MESS ... (A) ...... (B)	. (B)			(A) with Strap (B) with Cover.
BAGS, KIT ...	.			
KNIFE, CLASP, with } lanyard.	1			

Place *TEZZE* Signature of Soldier

Date *16-1-19*

Blou Boc R F A

Commanding.

(1857.) Wt. W 3094—P 1820. 250m. 8/18. D.& S. E 1266. Form W 3321/5.

Army Form W 3321.

Statement showing Articles of Clothing and Necessaries

IN POSSESSION OF

Regtl. No. *107274* Rank *GUNNER* Name *HERALY. A J*

Regiment *Blou Boc R.F.A.* Proceeding from *ITALY* to *ENGLAND*

	Mounted Services.	Dism'd Service (except Killed Regts.)	Killed Regts.	REMARKS.
BLANKETS, G.S. ...	3			
BOOTS, ANKLE, pairs ...	.			
BOOTS, F.S. (or SHOE } PACKS), pairs.	1			
SOLES, INNER, FOR } ANKLE BOOTS.	1			
BRASSARDS (for } R.A.M.C. only).	.			
CAP, SERVICE DRESS ...	1			
TAM O' SHANTER OR BALMORAL } BONNET, KHAKI.	.			
GREATCOAT, DRAB, } OR COAT WARM, M.S.	1			† Coat, British Warm for Cyclists.
DRAWERS, COTTON ...				
DRAWERS, WOOLLEN } OR SHORT KNICKERS.	.			
JACKET, SERVICE DRESS	1			
PANTALOONS, CORD ...	1			
PUTTEES, pairs ...	1			
TROUSERS, SERVICE } DRESS.	.			
KILT AND APRON ...				
WAISTCOAT, CARDIGAN	1			
TITLES FOR SHOUL- } DER STRAPS, sets.	1			
BADGE, CAP. ...	.			
BRACES, pair ...	1			
BRUSH, SHAVING ...	1			
BRUSH, TOOTH ...	1			
CAP, COMFORTER ...	1			

P.T.O.

E/1915/
Store

RECORD OFFICE,   Army Form W. 5112.

13 SEP 1920

WOOLWICH   191 .

Dear Sir,

I am directed to transmit the accompanying   1914-15 Star
                                    which has been awarded to you

in respect of your services with the

Royal Field Artillery

as Number *107274 Gnr A.J. Heraty*

I am to request that you will be so good as to acknowledge the receipt
of the decoration on the attached form, which is to be returned to the above
address in the enclosed addressed envelope, which needs no stamp.

                              I am,

                              Your obedient Servant,

Kindly note that the rank engraved
on the Decoration is the rank held
at the time of disembarkation.

                              i/c Records.

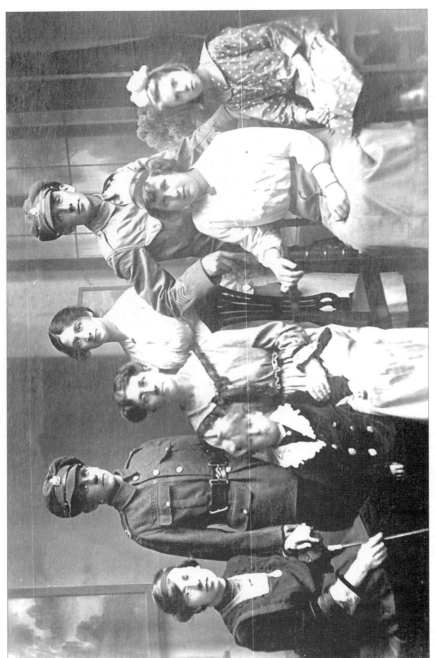

From left to right: Kate, John, Harold, my Mother, Annie, myself, Winnie and Cissy.

Epilogue

I was born Austin James Heraty, 2nd December 1896 at Prospect Terrace, Newcastle-under-Lyme, Staffordshire, one of eight children - Annie, Mary, Winnie, John, Kate, Cissy, Harold and myself - of Austin and Annie Heraty. My father was Assistant Headmaster at Wellington Road School, Hanley

I married Cissy Longshaw on June 23rd 1919 and we had six children - Kathleen, died aged 6, Joyce, Joan, Austin, Peter, died aged 3, and Anthony. After getting de-mobbed and married in 1919, I went back to working at Benzole House in Apedale, drawing gases off the coke ovens, until 1924. From there I went to work as a partner with

The retort house in a gasworks.

George Scott and Sons, in a small shop in Newcastle High Street until we moved to Merrial Street the next year, 1925, where I worked on crystal sets.

In 1928 I became unemployed, chopping sticks to earn a few bob. I then got a job working for Bob Berrisford, motor cycle and radio engineer, installing talking movies, which I did until 1933. From here I went to T. A. Knight, electrical and radio engineers in Stone until 1936, when I moved to a similar firm in Hanley working there through to 1941. From 1941 to 1945 I worked at Alcock's radio, gramophone and cycle specialists in Burslem.

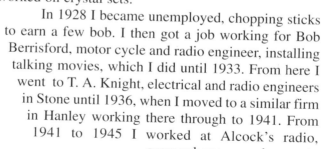

Radio Times 1925

THE CHILDREN'S SET.

R.I. **Permanent Mineral Detector Crystal Set.**

This wonderful little Set makes things

EVER SO EASY—There is only one knob to turn. No adjustment of any description. Perfect reception always.

Complete in polished mahogany cabinet. Price **£2-2-0.**

I was in the A.R.P. during the World War II and we all met at a public house in Orme Road, Pool Dam. My younger brother John served with the Royal Engineers and he was the soldier who blew the last retreat at Dunkirk. In 1945 I left Alcocks and joined a firm called John Ward, and for a short while I was rewiring surplus tanks left over from the War. The company closed down in the 1950s because they were selling tanks to the Israelis!

In 1946 I opened my own radio and T.V. shop in George Street. When I sold up in 1956, I went to work as a manager of three shops for T.V. Cadman of Hanley. When I was 60, in 1957, I went to work for Midland Mail at Fenwick for a couple of years, after which I had several small jobs - bakery lodgeman, petrol forecourt attendant, and I used to go around in a small van sharpening scissors, knives, mower blades - anything that wanted sharpening.

When I retired and got thinking about the Great War, my son Tony suggested I sit down and write my experiences. In 1979 I tried to get it published but the publishers said there would not be enough interest and it was too short.

Austin James Heraty died May 21st 1980 aged 83.

Our golden wedding anniversary, myself and my wife at the front. At the back, left to right, Joan, Tony, Joyce and, inset, Austin, who lives in Canada now.